No.1
BEST SELLER

AF674198

NCERT Notes

Indian Economy

Class 9-12 (Old+New)

No.1
BEST SELLER

NCERT Notes

Indian Economy

Class 9-12 (Old + New)

Authors
Ameebh Ranjan
Md. Fazle Kibria
Series Editor
Surya Singh

arihant
SUCCESS AND NOTHING LESS

arihant
SUCCESS AND NOTHING LESS

ARIHANT PUBLICATIONS (INDIA) LIMITED

Administrative & Production Offices

Regd. Office

'Ramchhaya' 4577/15, Agarwal Road, Darya Ganj, New Delhi -110002
Tele: 011- 47630600, 43518550

Head Office

Kalindi, TP Nagar, Meerut (UP) - 250002
Tel: 0121-7156203, 7156204

Sales & Support Offices

Agra, Ahmedabad, Bengaluru, Bareilly, Chennai, Delhi, Guwahati, Hyderabad, Jaipur, Jhansi, Kolkata, Lucknow, Nagpur & Pune.

PRICE ₹105.00

PO No : TXT-59-T069786-3-26

Published by Arihant Publications (India) Ltd.

For further information about the books published by Arihant, log on to www.arihantbooks.com or e-mail at info@arihantbooks.com

Follow us on

Two Words

NCERT are the Foundation in the Journey of IAS...

Civil Services Examinations are the most prestigious and coveted examinations in India. Being the toughest exam, it automatically consists of a vast and a detailed syllabus. Aspirants often find it difficult to cover the entire syllabus and lack a right direction for a proper and a systematic study for the exam.

The most important aspect of this preparation journey are the **NCERT books**. Every year approximately **35-40 questions** directly come from NCERT books.

NCERT books also play a key role in understanding the **Basic Concepts**; so that aspirants can easily form the basic foundation of the entire syllabus. But due to the demand for many NCERT books which are required for study, it becomes exhausting to cover each and every NCERT book.

NCERT NOTES SERIES presented by Arihant Publications covers complete text from Class 9th to 12th NCERT books in a comprehensive manner.

Features of Revised Edition

- Extra and relevant facts from exam point of view are covered from Tamil Nadu Board Books.
- Most important facts from NIOS books also compiled to enrich the content.
- Theory in each chapter is facilited with charts, tables, etc. to make the preparation easy and convenient.
- Exam focused last minute revision topics are also covered in the appendix.

The book is adorned with questions prepared by a team of experts along with a vital role played by the Project Management team with members: Mona Yadav (Project Manager), Sumit Verma (Project Coordinator), Seema Saini (Proof Reading TL), Pradeep Chaudhary (DTP TL), Bilal Hashmi, Rakesh Rawat and Ankit Tyagi (Cover and Inner designer).

We hope this book will help the aspirants to achieve their goals of clearing UPSC as well as State PCS exams. Your valuable suggestions have always inspired us to strive for useful, authentic and more trustworthy publications. So your inputs and suggestions are welcomed for subsequent editions.

We wish you all the very best for your preparation and journey!!

Authors

CONTENTS

INDIAN ECONOMY

01

Economy : An Introduction

[SOURCES]

Class-IX New NCERT Chap 1 (The Story of Village Palampur), Chap 2 (People as a Resource), Class-IX & X Old NCERT Chap 1 (An Overview of the Indian Economy), Class X New NCERT Chap 1 (Development), Chap 2 (Sectors of the Indian Economy), Class-XI New NCERT Chap 1 (Indian Economy on the Eve of Independence), Chap 2 (Indian Economy (1950-1990), Chap 4 (Human Capital Formation in India), Chap 7 (Environment and Sustainable Development), Class-XII New NCERT Chap 1 (Introduction) Tamil Nadu Board (Class-XII), NIOS

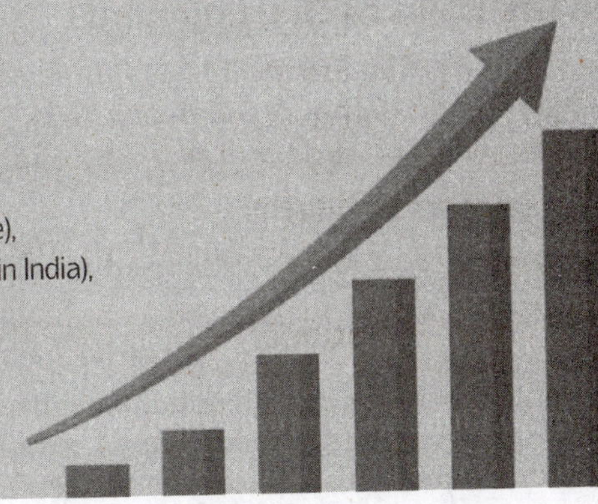

Economy : An Introduction

A framework in which all the economic activities are carried out in the form of investment, production and consumption, is termed as economy.

Types of Economy

Depending on the basis of classification, economies can be of various types as follows :

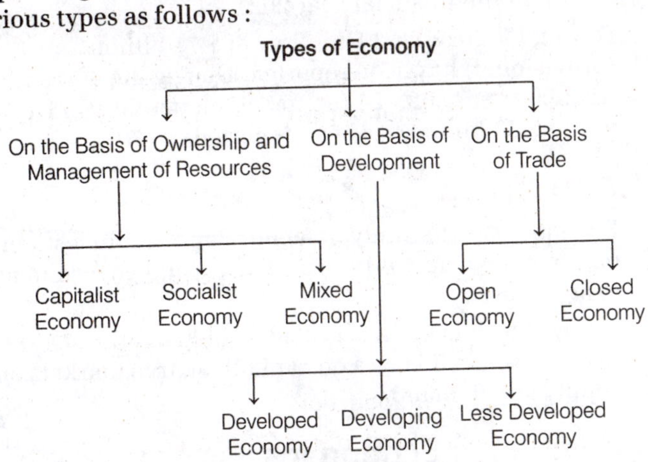

On the Basis of Ownership and Management of Resources

On the basis of ownership and management of resources, economies can be classified into Capitalist Economy, Socialist Economy and Mixed Economy.

1. Capitalist Economy

- In this type of economy, the private enterprises are the main spheres of production.
- They control the operation of the price mechanism by which buyers and sellers determine what goods and services will be bought and sold in the market.
- The means of production in the capitalist economy are controlled by private owners of capital, who operate for their private profit or gain.
- United States of America and United Kingdom are examples of capitalist economy.

2. Socialist Economy

- In this type of economy, there is existence of public enterprise or state ownership of capital in all the important spheres of productive activity.
- In the place of free operation of market forces, the socialist economies depend on state planning of production and distribution.
- China and Russia are examples of a socialist economy.

3. Mixed Economy

- In this type of economy, some of the important enterprises engaged in production are owned by the government but other enterprises have private owners.
- India is the example of a mixed economy.

India's Mixed Economy Model

- In India, all three sectors coexist in harmony, i.e. private sector, public sector and joint sector. The joint sector is jointly run by the government and private companies, with at least 51% ownership belonging to the state.
- The government can regulate and direct the working of private enterprise in India to safeguard public interest through different provisions of the law.

On the Basis of Development

On the basis of economic development, economies can be classified into Developed Economies, Developing Economies and Less Developed Economies.

1. Developed Economy

- It is also called an industrialised economy.
- This economy has advanced technological infrastructure and diverse industrial and service sectors.
- Countries which had been industrialised since long time like USA, UK, France, Japan, South Korea and other newly industrialised countries of Asia are the examples of developed economy.

2. Developing Economies

- In this type of economy, the modern industrial sector, keeps increasing in size and the traditional agricultural or rural sector keeps shrinking.
- It has a low socio-economic indicators and moderate Human Development Index as compared to other developed countries.
- China and India are the examples of developing economy.

3. Less Developed Economy

- According to the United Nations, this type of economy include developing economies that exhibit the lowest indicators of socio-economic development, with the lowest Human Development Index ratings of all countries in the world.
- The poorer countries are generally described as Less/Least Developed Countries (LDCs).
- They have relatively very small industrial sectors. They also have very little access to modern technology whether in industry or agriculture.
- Bangladesh, Niger, Central African Republic, South Sudan, Chad, Burundi, Sierra Leone, Burkina Faso, Mali, etc. are the examples of less developed economy.

On the Basis of Trade

On the basis of trade, economies can be divided into Open Economy and Closed Economy.

1. Open Economy

- It refers to a market economy, which is generally free from trade barriers and where exports and imports form a large percentage of the Gross Domestic Product (GDP).
- The degree of openness of an economy determines a government's freedom to pursue economic policies of its choice and the susceptibility of the country to international economic cycles.
- India after 1991 economic reforms, Chile and Argentina are the examples of open economy.

2. Closed Economy

- It refers to an economy in which no activity is conducted with other economies.
- It is self-sufficient, where no imports are brought in and no exports are sent out.
- The goal is to provide consumers with everything that they need from within the economy. India before 1991 economic reforms, is the example of closed economy.

Size of Indian Economy

- **As per 2023**, on the basis of economic indicators, India is **5th largest economy** of the world.
- On the basis of Purchasing Power Parity (PPP), India is **3rd largest economy** of the world after USA and China.
- According to UNCTAD (United Nations Conference on Trade and Development), World Investment Report 2023, India is world's 3rd largest hub for foreign investment in greenfield projects.
- FDI inflow in India stood at $36 billion in 2013-14 and registered its highest ever annual FDI inflow of $ 85 billion in the financial year 2021-22.
- During FY 2022-23, FDI inflow of $ 71 billion (provisional) has been reported. During the current financial year 2023-24 (up to September 2023) FDI worth $ 33 billion has been reported.

Economics

- Economics is the study of labour, land and investments of money, income, production, taxes and government expenditures.
- **Adam Smith** is known as 'Father of Economics'. Because of his theories on capitalism, free markets and supply and demand.

Activities in Economics

In order to fulfill desires of day-to-day life, people keep themselves engaged in different types of activities, which are as follows :

- **Economic Activities** The activities which create economic or financial gain by producing goods or services are known as economic activities. e.g., doctor, teacher, businessmen, etc.

- **Non-Economic Activities** The activities does not for earning money or any consideration of economic gain are known as non-economic activities. e.g., social services, political services, religious services, etc.

Branches of Economics

Economic analysis is usually divided into two main branches of economics i.e., Macroeconomics and Microeconomics.

- **Macroeconomics** It is concerned with problems of an economy as a whole rather than individual facts and problems. e.g., National Income, unemployment, poverty, balance of payments, inflation, etc.
- **Microeconomics** It studies economic activities at micro level. It examines the economic behaviour of individual units such as consumers, businessmen, etc to understand how decisions are made in the situation of scarcity and effects of these decisions on the economy. E.g. individual demand, individual supply, opportunity cost and consumer theory, etc.

Note *Microeconomics is known as price theory whereas macroeconomics is known as Income theory.*

Sectors of Economy

An economy is divided into three parts or sectors on the basis of economic activities. These activities are broadly grouped into Primary, Secondary and Tertiary sectors.

1. Primary Sector

- It is directly related to the extraction or utilisation of natural resources. It comprises economic activities like agriculture, mining, fishing, dairy, quarrying, etc.
- Products of primary sector does not undergo for major processing of change and are used or traded as natural products itself.
- This sector is also known as the **Agriculture and Allied Sector**.
- The Agriculture sector is at the third place with the contribution of 21.82% in GDP in 2022.

2. Secondary Sector

- It utilises the end product of the primary sector, to manufacture finished goods, through the refinement and processing of the primary products.
- It comprises construction, manufacturing, electricity, gas and water supply, etc related works.
- This sector is also known as the **Industrial Sector**.
- The Industry sector lags behind Service Sector with
- The contribution of 24.29% in GDP in 2022.

3. Tertiary Sector

- It provides services, instead of goods to other sectors. Thus, this sector is sometimes referred to as the **Service Sector**.
- Business, transport, telecommunication, banking, insurance, etc are associated with the sector.
- In India, the Service Sector accounts for almost 53.89% of India's GDP contribution in 2022.

Other Sectors of Economy

1. **Quaternary Sector** The quaternary sector consists of those industries providing information services, such as computing, ICT (Information and Communication Technologies), consultancy (offering advice to businesses) and Research and Development, particularly in scientific fields.
2. **Quinary Sector** Economists further narrow the quaternary sector into the quinary sector, which includes the highest levels of decision-making in a society or economy. This sector includes top executives or officials in such fields as government, science, universities, healthcare, culture and media.

Features of Indian Economy

The features of Indian economy can be categorised as traditional and modern features.

Traditional Features of Indian Economy

The traditional features of Indian economy are as follows:

1. Primacy of Agriculture

- Approx 45.5% of the working population of the country is engaged in agriculture and agriculture share in the Gross Domestic Product (GDP) is 18%.
- This share is one of the highest in India's Gross Domestic Product.
- In India, other sectors are also developing quiet fast, but agriculture still remains most employable sector of the country. Agriculture has 13.3% share in India's export.

2. Low Per Capita Income

- Low level of Per Capita Income is one of a major dilemma in the development of the country, because of increasing population and lower level of Per Capita Income, there is persistence of poverty in India.

3. Rural Economy

- According to Census 2011, 67% of India's population lives in rural areas which shows the rural population is quiet high.
- In developed economies, the percentage of rural population is quite low.

4. High Population

- Continuous and fast rising population makes the Indian economy weak.
- Between 2001 to 2011, the population rise in India was 17.64%.
- Due to rise in population, stress in the available resources is created.
- If a country has limited or less population, then there is a greater chances of decrease in social inequality that benefits larger masses.

5. Unemployment

- In India, there is a huge amount of workforce, but employment opportunities are few.
- In such a situation, it becomes very difficult to provide employment to everyone.
- Due to more population engaged in agriculture sector that is needed, it affects the productiveness of the country. In India, more human resource is engaged in agriculture than any other sectors.

6. Inequality in Income Distribution

- There is a huge inequality in distribution of income and property in India, that gives rise to problem of poverty and unemployment. Due to progressive taxation system in developed countries, there is low income inequalities.
- Equal opportunities of social security, education, training and employment decreases the scope of income inequality in an economy.

Modern Features of Indian Economy

The modern features of Indian economy are as follows :

1. Planned Economy

- In India, the phase of planned economy started from establishment of Planning Commission and preparing of Five Years Plan.
- In between 1951 and 2017, 12 Five Years Plan have been prepared so far.
- NITI Aayog was established on 1st January, 2015. At present, this organisation is responsible for preparing both short-term and long-term development plans.

2. Industrial Development

- In many Five Years Plans, establishment of industrial plans gave rise to the industrial development in India.
- In the year 1991, the process of liberalisation, privatisation and globalisation also began for development along with the initiation of 'New Economic Policies'. This gave rise to the industrial development in India.

Economic Development

In economic growth, the concept of social justice and fair distribution is termed as Economic Development. It is a qualitative concept.

Indicators of Economic Development

Alternative indicators have been developed by different national and international organisations to provide better measures of a nation's quality of life. These includes :

- The Human Development Index (HDI)
- Multi-dimensional Poverty Index (MPI)
- World Happiness Report (WHR)
- Gender Inequality Index (GII)
- Global Hunger Index (GHI)

Each of these indexes is a composite measure weighing both income and non-income variables such as life expectancy, literacy rates, environmental indicators, measures of inequality and so on. By including these variables, they provide a measure of life quality that goes beyond the narrowness of a nation's GDP value.

1. Human Development Index (HDI)

- The United Nations Development Programme (UNDP) introduced the HDI in its first Human Development Report (HDR), prepared under the stewardship of **Mahbub-ul-Haq** and Amartya Sen in 1990.
- HDR, 1990 defined human development as the process of widening people's choices as well as raising the level of well-being achieved.
- Three main indicators of HDI are as follows :
  - **Life Expectancy Index** (LEI) Infant mortality is not considered as a separate indicator in this index. Thus, life expectancy refers to life expectancy at birth, not at age one.
  - **Educational Attainment Index** (EAI) It is a combination of adult literacy rate and combined enrolment ratio. The weight assigned to Adult Literacy Rate (ALR) is two-third while for Combined Enrolment Ratio (CER) is one-third.
  - **Standard of Living Index** (SLI) It is represented here by the concept of Purchasing Power Parity (PPP). Per Capita Income is converted into Purchasing Power Parity in terms of US dollar. It is also known as **GDP Index**. The value of HDI is scaled on 1 to 0, where 1 represents the best and 0 (zero) represents the worst.

$$HDI = \frac{1}{3}(LEI + EAI + SLI)$$

2. Multi-dimensional Poverty Index (MPI)

- The Multi-dimensional Poverty Index was launched by the United Nations Development Programme (UNDP) and the Oxford Poverty and Human Development Initiative (OPHI) in 2010.
- MPI is based on the idea that poverty is not unidimensional (not just depends on income and one individual may lack several basic needs like education, health, etc.), rather it is multi-dimensional.
- The index shows the proportion of poor people and the average number of deprivations each poor person experiences at the same time.
- MPI uses three dimensions and ten indicators which are as follows :
  - **Education** Years of schooling and child enrollment.
  - **Health** Child mortality rate and nutrition.
  - **Standard of Living** Electricity, flooring, drinking water, sanitation, cooking fuel and assets.
- A person is multi-dimensionally poor if she/he is deprived in one-third or more (means 33% or more) of the weighted indicators (out of the ten indicators).
- Those who are deprived in one half or more of the weighted indicators are considered as living in extreme multi-dimensional poverty.

3. World Happiness Report (WHR)

- The phrase 'Gross National Happiness' was first coined by the fourth King of Bhutan, **King Jigme Singye Wangchuck**, in 1972.
- The concept implies that sustainable development should take a holistic approach towards notions of progress and give equal importance to non-economic aspects of wellbeing.
- The World Happiness Report ranks 146 countries by how happy their citizens perceive themselves to be.
- World Happiness Report is published by the United Nations' Sustainable Development Solutions Network.
- The rankings are based on polling (Gallup World Poll), which looks at six variables:
  (i) Gross Domestic Product Per Capita (Purchasing Power Parity)
  (ii) Social Support
  (iii) Healthy life expectancy at birth
  (iv) Freedom to make life choices
  (v) Generosity
  (vi) Perceptions of corruption

4. Gender Inequality Index (GII)

- GII is released by United Nations Development Programme (UNDP).
- It measures gender inequalities in following three important aspects of Human Development :
  (i) Reproductive health, measured by maternal mortality ratio and adolescent birth rates;
  (ii) Empowerment, measured by proportion of parliamentary seats occupied by females and proportion of adult females and males aged 25 years and older with at least some secondary education;
  (iii) Economic status, expressed as labour market participation and measured by labour force participation rate of female and male populations aged 15 years and older.

5. Global Hunger Index (GHI)

- This index is jointly published annually by **Concern Worldwide** and **Welthungerhilfe**.
- It was first prepared in 2006 and is published in every year in October. The 2023 edition marks the 18th edition of the GHI.
- It is calculated on the basis of four indicators :
  (i) **Under nourishment** Share of the population with insufficient caloric intake.
  (ii) **Child Wasting** Share of children under the age of five who have low weight for their height, reflecting acute undernutrition.
  (iii) **Child Stunting** Share of children under the age of five who have low height for their age, reflecting chronic undernutrition.
  (iv) **Child Mortality** The mortality rate of children under the age of five.
- Based on the values of the four indicators, the GHI determines hunger on a 100-point scale, where zero is the best possible score (no hunger) and 100 is the worst.
- Each country's GHI score is classified by severity, from low to extremely alarming.

Human Capital and Human Development

The two terms sound similar but there is a clear distinction between them.

Human Capital

- Population becomes human capital, when there is investment made in the form of education, training and medical care.
- Human capital considers education and health as a means to increase labour productivity.
- In fact, human capital is the stock of skill and productive knowledge embodied in them.
- 'People as Resource' is a way of referring to a country's working people in terms of their existing productive skills and abilities.

- When the existing 'human resource' is further developed by becoming more educated and healthy, we call it 'human capital formation' that adds to the productive power of the country just like 'physical capital formation'.

Sources of Human Capital

- Investment in education is considered as one of the main sources of human capital.
- There are also several other sources such as investments in health, on-the job training, migration and information are the other sources of human capital formation.

Difference Between Human Capital and Physical Capital

Physical Capital	Human Capital
Physical capital is tangible and can be easily sold in the market like any other commodity.	Human capital is intangible, it is endogenously built in the body and mind of its owner.
The physical capital is separable from its owner.	Human capital is inseparable from its owner.
Physical capital is completely mobile between countries except for some artificial trade restrictions.	Human capital is not perfectly mobile between countries as movement is restricted by nationality and culture.

Human Capital and Economic Growth

- Human capital allows an economy to grow. When human capital increases in areas such as science, education and management it leads to increase in innovation, social well-being, equality, increased productivity, improved rates of participation, etc. All of these contribute to economic growth.
- The causality between human capital and economic growth flows in either direction. That is, higher income causes the building of a higher level of human capital and vice-versa, that is, high level of human capital causes growth of income.
- India recognised the importance of human capital in economic growth long ago.
- The Seventh Five Year Plan says, "Human resources development has necessarily to be assigned a key role in any development strategy, particularly in a country with a large population."

Human Development

- Human development is based on the idea that education and health are integral to human well-being.
- Only when people have the ability to read and write alongwith the ability to lead a long and healthy life, then they will be able to make other choices, which they value.

Economic Growth

- It is an increase in the production of goods and services in an economy.
- It is a quantitative concept. It means an increase in real national income/national output.
- Increases in capital goods, labour force, technology, and human capital can contribute to the economic growth.
- Gross Domestic Product, Gross Value Added, Gross National Product, etc. are the measures of Economic Growth.

Comparative Analysis of Development of India and Its Neighbouring Countries

- India, Pakistan and China accepted same developmental policies.
- India announced its First Five Year Plan in 1951-56, Pakistan in 1956 and China in 1953.
- Important sectors, industries and land in China were brought under the control of the government.
- In 1958, China started **Great Leap Forward** programme which aimed at industrialisation at large scale.
- In rural areas, 'Commune' were started under this system, people practiced group farming. In 1966, Mao Zedong started 'Cultural Revolution' in China.
- In Pakistan, mixed economic model is practiced where both capitalist and socialist models coexist.
- In 1970s and 1980, Pakistan changed its policies but didn't gave emphasis on nationalisation. In 1970s, only industries of capital products were nationalised.
- At present time, most of the countries are promoting private sector.

Sustainable Development

- The term sustainable development is defined as "the development to achieve the needs of present generation without compromising future generation's needs."
- When the **World Commission on Environment and Development** (Brundtland Commission) published its report in 1987, it presented 'sustainable development' as a new concept.
- Sustainable development ensures the well-being of individuals by integrating social development, economic development, environmental conservation and protection.
- Sustainable Development Goals (SDGs) or Global Goals are a collection of **17 interlinked global goals** designed to be a 'blueprint to achieve a better and more sustainable future for all'.

- The SDGs were **set up in 2015** by the United Nations General Assembly and are intended to be achieved by the year 2030.

  These **17 goals** are as follows :

1. End poverty in all its forms everywhere.
2. End hunger, achieve food security and improved nutrition and promote sustainable agriculture.
3. Ensure healthy lives and promote well-being for all at all ages.
4. Ensure inclusive and equitable quality education and promote lifelong learning opportunities to all.
5. Achieve gender equality and empower all women and girls.
6. Ensure availability and sustainable management of water and sanitation for all.
7. Ensure access to affordable, reliable, sustainable and modern energy for all.
8. Promote sustained inclusive and sustainable economic growth, full and productive employment and decent work for all.
9. Build resilient infrastructure, promote inclusive and sustainable industrialisation and foster innovation.
10. Reduce inequality within and among countries.
11. Make cities and human settlements inclusive, safe, resilient and sustainable.
12. Ensure sustainable consumption and production patterns.
13. Take urgent action to combat climate change and its impacts.
14. Conserve and sustainably use the oceans, seas and marine resources for sustainable development.
15. Protect, restore and promote sustainable use of terrestrial ecosystems, sustainably manage forests, combat desertification and halt or reverse land degradation and halt biodiversity loss.
16. Promote peaceful and inclusive societies for sustainable development, provide access to justice for all and build effective, accountable and inclusive institutions at all.
17. Strengthen the means of implementation and revitalise the global partnership for sustainable development.

Extra Facts From Tamil Nadu Board and NIOS

- The term or word **Economics** comes from the Ancient Greek oikonomia (oikos means 'households' and, nemein means 'management', 'custom' or 'law'). Thus, the term 'Economics' means 'management of households'.

Difference between Public goods and Private goods

Public Goods	Private Goods
• A goods available to everyone to consume, regardless of who pays and who doesn't.	• A goods consumed by a single person or household.
• Spillover benefits.	• No spillover benefits.
• Non-rival in consumption and non-excludable.	• Rival in consumption and excludable.
• E.g. : National defence, Law enforcement.	• E.g. : food and drink

- **Engel's Law** The proportion of total expenditure incurred on food items declines as total expenditure goes on increasing.
- **Physical Quality of Life Index** (PQLI) It was developed by Morris David Morris. Based on three indicators such as life expectancy, infant mortality rate and literacy rate, it measures the quality of life.

02

National Income and Accounting

[SOURCES]

Class-X New NCERT Chap 1 (Development), Class-XI New NCERT Chap 1 (Indian Economy on the Eve of Independence), Class-XI Old NCERT Chap 2 (Accounting of National Income), Class-XII New NCERT Chap 2 (National Income Accounting), Class-XII Old NCERT Chap 3 (Accounting of National Income : Concepts and Measurement) Tamil Nadu Board (Class-XII), NIOS

National Income

National Income refers to the complete value of the final goods and services produced by any country during its financial year.

Thus, it is the consequence of all economic activities that are running in any country during the period of one year. It is valued in terms of money.

Historical Timeline of India's National Income

- The first attempt to calculate the National Income was made in 1868 by Dadabhai Naoroji in his book *'Poverty and Un-British Rule in India'*, who estimated the Per Capita Income at ₹ 20.
- Another effort was made by Dr. Vijayendra Kasturi Ranga Varadraja Rao, who was the first to use scientific approach to calculate National Income. In 1925 to 1929, he estimated Per Capita Income at ₹ 76.
- The Government of India appointed a National Income Committee under the Chairmanship of Dr. PC Mahalanobis. This committee gave its first report in 1951 and final report in 1954. The committee estimated *National Income* of ₹ 8650 crore and *Per Capita Income* of ₹ 246.50.

Basic Terms

- **Final Goods** Such goods that are meant for final use and will not pass through any more stages of production or transformations.
- **Consumption Goods** Goods like food and clothing and services like recreation that are consumed when purchased by their ultimate consumers are called consumption goods.
- **Capital Goods** Goods that are of durable character which are used in the production process. These are tools, implements and machines. While they make production of other commodities feasible, they themselves don't get transformed in the production phase.
- **Intermediate Goods** Such goods are used by other producers as material inputs. These are mostly used as raw material or inputs for production of other commodities.
- **Depreciation** It represents how much of an assets value has been used. It is an annual allowance for wear and tear of capital goods. In other words, it is the cost of the goods divided by the number of years of its useful life. Depreciation does not take into account unexpected or sudden destruction or disuse of capital as can happen with accidents, natural calamities or other such extraneous circumstances.
- **Market Price** It refers to the actual transacted price and it includes indirect taxes such as excise duty, Value Added Tax (VAT), service tax, customs duty, etc and government subsidies.
- **Factor Cost** It means the total cost of all factors of production consumed or used in producing a good or service. It includes government grants and subsidies, but it excludes indirect taxes.

- **Purchasing Power Parity** (PPP) It is an analysis metric to compare economic productivity and standards of living between two different countries. The PPP exchange rates are constructed to ensure that the same quantity of goods and services are priced equivalently across countries.
- **Base Year** It is the year against which the performance of an index is measured. It is also called the **reference year**.
- **Hindu Growth Rate** Professor **Rajkrishna**, an Indian economist, coined the term 'Hindu Growth Rate'. The Hindu rate of growth is a term referring to the low annual growth rate of the planned economy of India before the liberalisation of 1991.

Circular Flow of Income in a Simple Economy

- In Simple economy, factors of production use their remunerations to buy the goods and services which they assisted in producing.
- The aggregate consumption by the households of the economy is equal to the aggregate expenditure on goods and services produced by the firms in the economy.
- The entire income of the economy, therefore, comes back to the producers in the form of sales revenue.

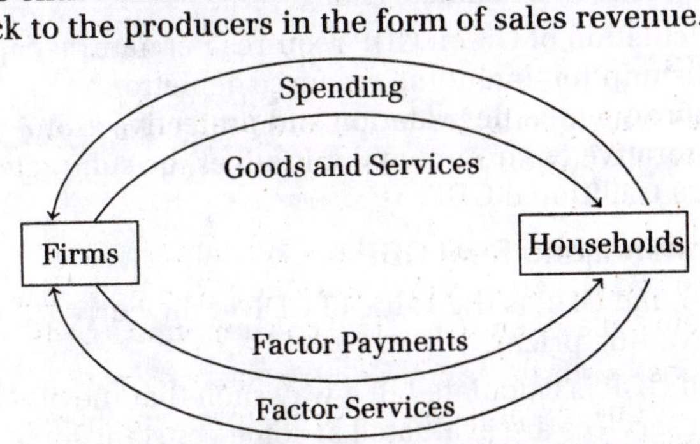

Circular Flow of Income in a Simple Economy

Calculation of National Income

- National Income (NI) measures the net value of goods and services produced in a country during a year and it also includes Net Factor Income from Abroad (NFIA).
- National Income measures the productive power of an economy in a given period to turn out goods and services for final consumption. In India, National Income estimates are related to the financial year (1st April to 31st March).
- According to the **National Income Committee** (1949), National Income estimate measures the volume of commodities and services turned out during a given period without duplication.

$$\text{National Income} = C + I + G + (X - M)$$

Where, C = Total Consumption Expenditure
I = Total Investment Expenditure
G = Total Government Expenditure
X = Export, M = Import

Various Measures of National Income

Economists use many methods to study National Income. Few of them are as follows :

1. Gross Domestic Product (GDP)

It measures the monetary value of all the final goods and services taking place within the domestic territory (within the borders of a country) during a year.

$$\text{GDP} = C + I + G$$

Where, C = Total Consumption Expenditure
I = Total Investment Expenditure
G = Total Government Expenditure

GDP at Market Price (GDP_{MP})

- It refers to the total value of all the goods and services at market price produced during a year within the geographical boundaries of the country.
- Market price refers to the actual transacted price and it includes indirect taxes such as Excise duty, VAT, Service tax, Customs duty, etc and government subsidies. That's why the GDP_{MP} (in ₹) has steadily increased in the last decades.

$$GDP_{MP} = GDP_{FC} + (\text{Indirect Taxes} - \text{Subsidies})$$

GDP at Factor Cost (GDP_{FC})

- GDP at factor cost is the total value of goods and commodities produced in a year in a country by its all production units (factory level). It includes government grants and subsidies, but it excludes indirect taxes.

$$GDP_{FC} = GDP_{MP} - \text{Indirect Tax} + \text{Subsidy}$$

Calculation of GDP in India

- GDP in a country is usually calculated by the **National Statistical Agency**, which compiles the information from a large number of sources.
- In the case of India, it is the National Statistics Office (NSO), which estimates GDP.
- The international standards for measuring GDP are obtained from the System of National Accounts, 1993, compiled by the International Monetary Fund (IMF), the European Commission (EC), the Organisation for Economic Cooperation and Development (OECD), the United Nations (UN) and the World Bank.

2. Gross Value Added (GVA)

- In 2015, India opted to make major changes to its compilation of national accounts and decided to bring the whole process into conformity with the United Nation's **System of National Accounts** (SNA) of 2008.
- As per the SNA, GVA is defined as the value of output minus the value of intermediate consumption and it is a measure of the contribution to growth made by an individual producer, industry or sector.
- It provides the rupee value for the number of goods and services produced in an economy after deducting the cost of inputs and raw materials that have gone into the production.

$$\text{GVA} = \text{GDP} + \text{Subsidies on Products} - \text{Taxes on Products}$$

- Earlier, India had been measuring GVA at 'factor cost' till the new methodology was adopted, in which GVA at 'basic prices' became the primary measure of economic output.
- GVA at basic prices will include production taxes and exclude production subsidies. GVA at factor cost included no taxes and excluded no subsidies.
- The base year from 2004-2005 has also been shifted to 2011-2012.

3. Gross National Product (GNP)

- It counts all the output of the residents/nationals of a country. So, if an Indian owned company has a factory in the United Kingdom, the output of that factory would be included in UK GDP, not in Indian GDP.
- However, while measuring GNP, the output of the Indian owned factory in the UK would be included in India's GNP.
- Thus, while calculating GNP, the Net Factor Income from Abroad will be included.

$$\text{GNP}_{(FC/MP)} = \text{GDP}_{(FC/MP)} + X - I$$

Where,

X = Income Earned and Received by Indians Working Abroad

I = Income Earned and Received by Non-Indians in India

4. Net Domestic Product (NDP)

- If the depletion of the capital stock (Depreciation), is subtracted from GDP, Net Domestic Product (NDP) is obtained. The difference between Gross and Net Domestic Product occurs because of depreciation.
- In terms of value addition, the summation of Net Value Added (NVA) of all firms is called Net Domestic Product (NDP).

$$\text{NDP}_{(FC/MP)} = \text{Gross Domestic Product}_{(FC/MP)} - \text{Depreciation}$$

5. Net National Product (NNP)

If we deduct depreciation from GNP, the measure of aggregate income will give NNP.

$$\text{NNP}_{(FC/MP)} = \text{Gross National Product}_{(FC/MP)} - \text{Depreciation}$$

Note *NNP at factor cost gives us the Real National Income of India.*

6. Per Capita Income (PCI)

- Per Capita Income (PCI) measures the average income earned per person in a given area (city, region, country, etc.) in a specified year.
- It is calculated by dividing the area's total income by its total population. Per Capita Income is National Income divided by population size.

$$\text{Per Capita Income (PCI)} = \text{National Income/Total Population}$$

7. Green Gross Domestic Product (GGDP)

- It is an index of economic growth with the environmental consequences of that growth factored into a country's conventional GDP. Green GDP monetises the loss of biodiversity and accounts for costs caused by climate change.
- Calculation of Green GDP requires net natural capital consumption including resource depletion, environmental degradation and protective and restorative environmental initiatives, be subtracted from traditional GDP.

8. Nominal and Real GDP

- Nominal GDP is the value of GDP at the current prevailing prices.
- Real GDP is calculated in a way such that the goods and services are evaluated at some constant set of prices. Since these prices remain fixed, if the real GDP-changes we can be sure that it is the volume of production which is undergoing changes.

9. GDP Deflator

- The ratio of nominal to real GDP is a Index of prices.
- The ratio of nominal GDP to real GDP gives us an idea of how the prices have moved from the base year to the current year.

$$\text{GDP deflator} = \frac{\text{GDP}}{\text{gdp}} \times 100$$

Where, GDP = Nominal GDP, gdp = Real GDP

Various Methods of Measuring National Income

According to **Simon Kuznets,** National Income Accounting of a country is calculated by the following three methods :

1. Product Method

- This method of National Income Accounting calculates the aggregate value of final goods and services produced in a year.

GDP = Value of Output – Intermediate Consumption

- The Gross Domestic Product (GDP) of an economy is arrived at by measuring the aggregate value of goods and services produced in a year.
- Further deducting the aggregate amount of depreciation, across all firms in an economy, gives us the Net Domestic Product (NDP).

2. Income Method

- In this method, a sum of net income earned by working people in different sectors and commercial enterprises is obtained. Incomes of both categories of people, tax-paying and non-tax-paying, are added to obtain National Income.
- It is calculated by measuring the aggregate level of income, rent, interest and profits by the respective factors of production of an economy.

National Income (NI) = (Total rent – Income from land) + (Total wages – Income from labour) + (Total interest – Income from capital) + (Total profit – Income from entrepreneur).

3. Consumption Method

- In this method, income is either spent on consumption or saved.
- Hence, National Income is the addition of total consumption and total savings. It is also called the **Expenditure Method**.

NI = Total Consumption Expenditure + Total Savings

Organisations Associated With National Income Calculation in India

Organisation	Description
Central Statistical Organisation (CSO)	It was a governmental agency in India under the Ministry of Statistics and Programme Implementation responsible for coordination of statistical activities in India, and evolving and maintaining statistical standards.
National Sample Survey Office (NSSO)	It was set-up in 1950 on the recommendation of Dr. PC Mahalanobis, for conducting large-scale sample surveys to meet the data needs of the country, for the estimation of National Income and other aggregates.
National Statistical Office (NSO)	The government has merged the Central Statistical Organisation (SO) and National Sample Survey Organisation (NSSO) under the Ministry of Statistics and Programme Implementation (MOSPI) into a single entity on 23rd May, 2019.
National Statistical Commission (NSC)	It was established on 1st June, 2005 based on the recommendations of Rangarajan Committee (2000) to reduce the problems faced by statistical agencies in the country in relation to collection of data.

Extra Facts From Tamil Nadu Board and NIOS

Nobel laureate Simon Kuznets First introduced the concept of national income.

- **Factor Cost** It refer to the cost of production that is incurred by a firm when producing goods and services. It include things such as land, labour, capital and entrepreneurship.
- **Private Income** Consists of factor incomes earned within the domestic territory and abroad by private enterprises and workers and current transfer from government and the rest of the world.
- **Private Income** = Income from domestic product accruing to private sector + Net factor income from abroad + national debt interest + current transfers from government + other current transfers from the rest of the world (net).
- **Personal Income** It is defined as the current income of persons or households from all sources.
- **Personal Income** = Private income – saving of private corporate sector (undistributed profit) – corporation tax
- **Personal Disposable Income** It is the income available to persons from all sources to dispose of as they choose.
- **Personal Disposable Income** = Personal income – direct taxes paid by the households – miscellaneous receipts of the government.
- **National Income** It is also being measured by the social accounting method. Under this method, the transactions among various sectors such as firms, households, government, etc., are recorded and their inter-relationships traced.
- **National Disposable Income** It refers to the income which is available to the whole country for disposable. It includes both earned income and transfer income (unearned income).

Net National Disposable Income = NNPmp + Net current transfers from rest of the world.

- **Difficulties in measuring national income:**
  1. Transfers payments
  2. Difficulties in assessing depreciation allowance
  3. Unpaid services
  4. Income from illegal activities
  5. Production for self-consumption and changing price
  6. Capital gains
  7. Statistical problems

03

Economic Planning

[SOURCES]

Class-IX New NCERT Chap 2 (People As a Resource),
Class-IX & X Old NCERT Chap 5 (The State and Economic Development),
Class-XI New NCERT Chap 2 (Indian Economy 1950-1990)
Tamil Nadu Board (Class-XII), NIOS

Planning in Indian Economy

- Economic planning refers to the path of actions in terms of policy measures to be followed in future, for pursuing pre-determined objectives. It is a consciously and judiciously carried out process for optimum utilisation of existing resources in order to fulfil some well-defined objectives.
- The **Planning Commission** defined economic planning as "the utilisation of a country's resources for developmental activities in accordance with national priorities."
- Under the Indian Constitution, economic planning is headed in the 7th Schedule and under Concurrent list. The economic planning in India is based on mix of capitalist and socialist economy model.

Objectives of Planning in India

- The fundamental objective of planning in India is to achieve an increase in National Income and Per Capita Income.
- Another objective of planning is to improve agricultural production for achieving self-sufficiency in foodgrains production.

  Other objectives of economic planning are as follows :
  - Meeting the needs of industry and export.
  - Achieve industrialisation with special reference to basic and heavy industries.
  - Provide more employment opportunities.
  - Reduce inequalities in income and wealth distribution.
  - Achieve self-reliance and eradicate poverty to achieve economic growth.

History of Planning in India

For planned development, many plans, proposal, reforms, etc were passed in India. Some of these are discussed as follows:

Visvesvaraya Plan

- First systematic work on planning came into existence in the year 1934 when renowned engineer and statesmen **M. Visvesvaraya** formulated a Ten Year Plan for economic development.
- He amalgamated his plan in his book **'Planned Economy for India'**.
- He emphasised on increasing the industrial production and coordinated development of small and large enterprises.

FICCI's Proposal

- In 1934, Federation of India Chambers of Commerce and Industry (FICCI) emphasised on economic planning in India.
- It was the first formal organisation by Indian industrialists, under the Chairmanship of **NR Sarkar**.
- He recommended that country like India should have a comprehensive economic planning.

National Planning Committee

- In 1938, Congress President and Indian National Army supreme leader **Netaji Subhash Chandra Bose** initiated planning in India under the Chairmanship of **Jawaharlal Nehru**.
- This was followed by the formation of a 15 members of National Planning Committee.
- The Committee emphasised that the national independence is a primary condition for taking all the steps that might be found necessary for carrying out planning.
- The National Planning Committee appointed several sub-committees to study different aspects of the national economy.

Gandhian Strategy

- It was proposed by **Shriman Narayan Agarwal** in 1944.
- It emphasised on the economic decentralisation with primary to rural development by developing cottage industries.

Bombay Plan

- In early 1944, industrialists and economists of Bombay, **Sir Purshottamdas Thakurdas, Mr. JRD Tata** and six others attempted and published a development plan.
- Its main objective was doubling the per capita income in the country over a period of 15 years.
- It proposed an increase of about 130% and 500% in agriculture and industry respectively. The total outlay of ₹ 10,000 crores was recommended.

People's Plan

- It was a Ten Year Plan prepared by **MN Roy** in 1945.
- Its emphasis was on agriculture and consumer goods industries through collectivisation and setting up of state owned industrialisation.
- It advocated nationalisation of land with the total outlay of ₹ 15000 crores.

Sarvodaya Plan

- It was drafted by **Jaiprakash Narayan** in 1950. It was inspired by Gandhian Plan and Sarvodaya idea of **Vinoba Bhave**.
- It suggested the freedom from foreign technology and stressed upon land reforms and decentralised participatory planning.

LPG Reforms

- The government announced a **New Economic Policy** on 24th July, 1991. It is commonly known as Liberalisation, Privatisation and Globalisation model.
- The plan's objective was to put India's economy into the area of globalisation. It ended the licence/permit raj for maximum industries.

Types of Planning

Planning can be classified as follows :

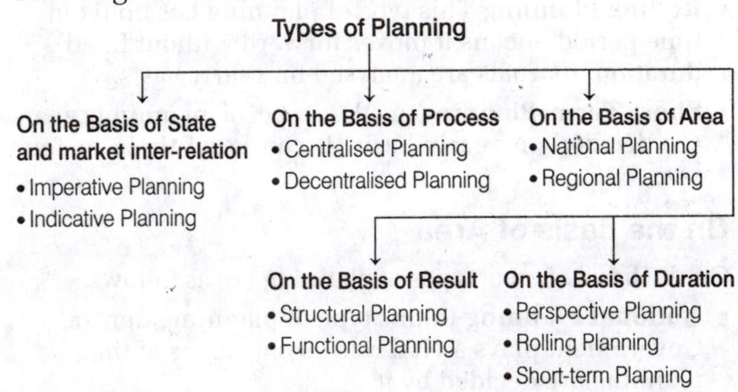

On the Basis of State and Market Inter-relation

On the basis of state and market inter-relation, types of planning are as follows :

- **Imperative Planning** A socialist planning is called imperative planning as the central planning authority performs all economic activities in the best interests of the society.
- **Indicative Planning** In this type of planning, all policies of the country operate under the direction of government. Role of state is only a motivating and promoting factor in policies.

On the Basis of Result

On the basis of result, types of planning are as follows :

- **Structural Planning** In this type of planning the present social and economic structure is changed and a new structure emerges.
- **Functional Planning** The functional plans could be considered an overall strategy or plan describing how, when and where the objectives and goals will be accomplished for each function as well as for the entire plan.

On the Basis of Process

On the basis of process, types of planning are as follows :

- **Centralised Planning** In this type of planning, all the economic decisions are taken by the Central Government. It is also known as Top-to-bottom planning.
- **Decentralised Planning** It is a kind of percolation of planning activities or processes from the centre to the sub-state levels, i.e., district, sub-division, block and village level.

On the Basis of Duration

On the basis of duration, types of planning are as follows :

- **Perspective Planning** It refers to long-term planning, in which a long range of targets are set in advance for a period of 15, 20 or 25 years. e.g., Vision 2020, National Population Policy (NPP) 2000, etc.
- **Rolling Planning** This type of planning has no fixed time period, means it moves forward without fixed duration. Its goals are analysed on yearly basis.
- **Short-Term Planning** In this type of planning, goals are decided on yearly basis. It can be of three or four years.

On the Basis of Area

On the basis of area, types of planning are as follows :

- **National Planning** In this type of planning, Central Government plays a vital role as objectives of the planning are decided by it.
- **Regional Planning** The plan that aims to target a specific region for inclusive development and to reduce the regional imbalance is called regional planning. The Eighth Five-Year Plan specified the programme of the special area such as Hilly areas North-Eastern state development, tribal areas and backward areas development.

Planning Commission

- The Planning Commission of India was set up by a Resolution of the Government of India on 15th March, 1950.
- Institutionally, it was a part of the Cabinet organisation and the 'demands for grants' for the Planning Commission were included in the budget for the Cabinet Secretariat.
- It was a non-constitutional body. Its first chairman (Ex-officio) was Jawaharlal Nehru (The then Prime Minister of India). Its first Deputy Chairman was **Gulzarilal Nanda**.

National Development Council (NDC)

- It was set up on 6th August, 1952. It was a non-constitutional and non-statutory body and also known as **Rashtriya Vikas Parishad**.
- NDC's objective was to strengthen and mobilise the effort and resources of the nation in support of the plan.
- It was presided over by the Prime Minister of India and included all Union Ministers, Chief Ministers of all the States, Administrators of Union Territories and Members of the Planning Commission.
- Ministers of State with independent charge were also invited for the deliberations of the Council.

NITI Aayog

- The Planning Commission was replaced by a new institution called NITI Aayog on 1st January, 2015 with emphasis on 'Bottom –Up' approach to envisage the vision of Maximum Governance, Minimum Government, echoing the spirit of 'Cooperative Federalism'.

Administrative structure of NITI Aayog

- **Chairperson** Prime Minister
- **Vice-Chairperson** To be appointed by Prime Minister
- **Governing Council** Chief Ministers of all states and Lt. Governors of Union Territories
- **Regional Council** To address specific regional issues, comprising Chief Ministers and Lt. Governors Chaired by the Prime Minister or his nominee
- **Adhoc Membership** Two members in ex-officio capacity from leading Research institutions on rotational basis
- **Ex-Officio Membership** Maximum four members from the Union Council of Ministers to be nominated by the Prime Minister
- **Chief Executive Officer** Appointed by Prime Minister for a fixed tenure, in rank of Secretary to Government of India
- **Special Invitees** Experts, Specialists with domain knowledge nominated by the Prime Minister

Objectives and Functions of NITI Aayog

The following are the objectives and functions of NITI Aayog :

- To foster cooperative federalism through structured support initiatives and mechanisms with the states on a continuous basis, recognising that strong states make a strong nation.
- To develop mechanisms to formulate credible plans at the village level and aggregate these progressively at higher levels of government.
- To ensure, on areas that are specifically referred to it, that the interests of National Security are incorporated in economic strategy and policy.
- To pay special attention to the sections of our society that may be at risk of not benefitting adequately from economic progress.
- To provide advice and encourage partnerships between key stakeholders and national and international like-minded Think Tanks, as well as educational and policy research institutions.
- To create a knowledge, innovation and entrepreneurial support system through a collaborative community of national and international experts, practitioners and other partners.

- To offer a platform for resolution of inter-sectoral and inter-departmental issues in order to accelerate the implementation of the development agenda.
- To maintain a state-of-the-art resource centre, be a repository of research on good governance and best practices in sustainable and equitable development as well as help their dissemination to stake-holders.

Five Year Plans in India

- After independence, India launched a programme of Five Year Plans which were **borrowed from** the former Soviet Union (now Russia) to make the optimum use of the country's available resources and to achieve rapid economic development.
- In India, development plans were formulated and carried out within the framework of the mixed economy.
- Our plan documents **upto the year 2017** not only specify the objectives to be attained in the five years of a plan but also, what is to be achieved over a period of 20 years.
- The Five Year Plans were supposed to provide the basis for the prospective plan.

The following gives us a description about the Five Year Plans (FYPs) in India:

1. First Five Year Plan (1951-1956)

- It was based on the **Harrod-Domar Model** with a few modifications. Its main focus was on the agricultural development of the country.
- This plan was successful and achieved a growth rate of 3.6% (more than its target of 2.1%).
- At the end of this plan, five IITs were set up in the country.

Harrod-Domar Model

- This strategy emphasised the role of capital accumulation's dual character, which on the one hand, increases the national income and on the other hand, increases the production capacity.
- According to this growth model, the rate of economic growth in an economy is dependent on the level of savings and capital output ratio.
- Rate of growth (Y) = Savings (S)/Capital output ratio (K)

2. Second Five Year Plan (1956-1961)

- It was based on the **PC Mahalanobis Model.**
- Its main focus was on the industrial development of the country.
- This plan lags behind its target growth rate of 4.5% and achieved a growth rate of 4.27%.

Mahalanobis Model

- This strategy was based on the two sector model-consumer goods sector and capital goods sector.
- The strategy emphasised investment in heavy industry to achieve industrialisation for rapid economic development. It was based on the Russian experience.
- This strategy was adopted in the Second Five Year Plan and with minor modifications, continued upto the Fifth Plan. It was a long-term strategy.

3. Third Five Year Plan (1961-1966)

- This plan is also called 'Gadgil Yojana', after the name of Deputy Chairman of Planning Commission Dr. Gadgil.
- The main target of this plan was to make the economy independent. The stress was laid on agriculture and the improvement in the production of wheat.
- During the execution of this plan, India was engaged in two wars:
  - The Sino-India War of 1962
  - The Indo-Pakistani War of 1965
- These wars exposed the weakness in our economy and shifted the focus to the defence industry, the Indian Army and the stabilisation of the price (India witnessed inflation). The plan was a flop due to wars and drought. The target growth was 5.6% while the achieved growth was 2.4%.

Plan Holidays (1966-1969)

- Due to the failure of the previous plan, the government announced three annual plans called Plan Holidays from 1966-1969.
- The main reason behind the failure of the Third Five Year Plan was the Indo-Pakistani War and the Sino-India War, leading to the plan holidays.
- During this plan, annual plans were made and equal priority was given to agriculture, its allied sectors and the industry sector.
- In a bid to increase the exports in the country, the government declared devaluation of the rupee.

4. Fourth Five Year Plan (1969-1974)

- There were two main objectives of this plan i.e. growth with stability and progressive achievement of self-reliance.
- During this time, 14 major Indian Banks were nationalised and the Green Revolution was started. The Indo-Pakistani War of 1971 and the Bangladesh Liberation War also took place.

- Implementation of Family Planning Programmes was amongst major targets of the Plan.
- This plan failed and could achieve a growth rate of 3.3% only against the target of 5.7%.

5. Fifth Five Year Plan (1974-1978)

- This plan focussed on **Garibi Hatao**, employment, justice, agricultural production and defence.
- In 1975, the Electricity Supply Act was amended, a Twenty-Point Programme (TPP) was launched, the Minimum Needs Programme (MNP) and the Indian National Highway System was also introduced at the same time.
- Overall this plan was successful, which achieved a growth of 4.8% against the target of 4.4%.
- This plan was terminated in 1978 by the newly elected Morarji Desai government.
- After the termination of the Fifth Five Year Plan, the Rolling Plan came into effect.

Rolling Plan

- This plan came into effect from 1978 to 1980.
- Three plans were introduced under the Rolling Plan
  - For the budget of the present year.
  - This plan was for a fixed number of years - 3, 4 or 5 years.
  - Perspective plan for long-terms - 10, 15 or 20 years.
- The plan has several advantages as the targets could be mended and projects, allocations, etc were variable to the country's economy.
- This means that, if the targets can be amended each year, it would be difficult to achieve the targets and will result in destabilisation in the Indian economy.
- In 1980, Congress rejected the Rolling Plan and a new **Sixth Five Year Plan** was introduced.

6. Sixth Five Year Plan (1980-1985)

- The basic objective of this plan was economic liberalisation by eradicating poverty and achieving technological self-reliance.
- It was based on investment, infrastructural development and focus on the growth model.
- Its growth target was 5.2% and it achieved 5.7% growth.

7. Seventh Five Year Plan (1985-1990)

- The objectives of this plan include the establishment of a self-sufficient economy, opportunities for productive employment and upgradation of technology.
- The plan aimed at accelerating food grain production, increasing employment opportunities and raising productivity with a focus on 'food, work and productivity'. For the first time, the private sector got priority over the public sector.
- Its growth target was 5.0% and it achieved 6.01%.

Annual Plans

- The Eighth Five Year Plan could not take place due to the volatile political situation at the centre.
- Two annual programmes were formed for the year 1990-1991 and 1991-1992.

8. Eighth Five Year Plan (1992-1997)

- In this plan, the top priority was given to the development of human resources i.e. employment, education and public health.
- During this plan, Narasimha Rao Government launched the New Economic Policy of India.
- Some of the main economic outcomes during the Eighth Five Year Plan period were rapid economic growth (highest annual growth rate so far – 6.8 %), high growth of agriculture and allied sector, manufacturing sector, growth in exports and imports, improvement in trade and current account deficit.
- A high growth rate was achieved even though the share of the public sector in total investment had declined considerably to about 34%.

9. Ninth Five Year Plan (1997-2002)

- The main focus of this plan was **'Growth with Social Justice and Equality'**.
- It was launched in the 50th year of Independence of India.
- This plan failed to achieve the growth target of 6.5% and achieved a growth rate of 5.6%.

10. Tenth Five Year Plan (2002-2007)

- This plan aimed to double the Per Capita Income of India in the next 10 years.
- It also aimed to reduce the poverty ratio to 15% by 2012.
- Its growth target was 8.0% but it achieved only 7.6%.

11. Eleventh Five Year Plan (2007-2012)

- It was prepared by the **C. Rangarajan**.
- Its main theme was 'Rapid and Inclusive growth'.
- It achieved a growth rate of 8% against a target of 9% growth.

12. Twelfth Five Year Plan (2012-2017)

- Its main theme is 'Faster, More Inclusive and Sustainable Growth' achievement.
- Its growth rate target was 8% but it achieved only 7.1% approx.

Five Year's Plan : At a Glance

Plan	Growth Rate	Achieved Growth Rate	Special Preferences/Programmes
First Five Year Plan (Harrod Domar Model)	2.1	3.6	• Agriculture and related Community Development Programme
Second Five Year Plan (Mahalanobis Model)	4.5	4.21	• Heavy industries, Health and Medical • Rourkela, Bhilai and Durgapur Steel Plants established
Third Five Year Plan (Gadgil Yojana)	5.6	2.72	• Food and Agriculture
Fourth Five Year Plan (DP Dhar Model)	5.7	3.3	• Agriculture and irrigation • Development with the aim of achieving stability and self-sufficiency
Fifth Five Year Plan	4.4	4.83	• Public health and Social welfare • Slogan of poverty eradication and self-reliance
Sixth Five Year Plan	5.2	5.4	• Agriculture, industry, power • Relentless plan • Poverty eradication
Seventh Five Year Plan	5.0	6.0	• Power and food
Eighth Five Year Plan	5.6	6.68	• Human Resource (Education, health employment) development
Ninth Five Year Plan	6.5	5.4	• Social justice, Rural development, Job creation • Growth with equitable distribution or equality
Tenth Five Year Plan	8.0	7.8	• Development of social infrastructure, employment and energy
Eleventh Five Year Plan	8.1	7.9	• Rapid economic growth, Job creation • Availability of basic physical and educational services
Twelfth Five Year Plan	8.0	7.1 (Approx.)	• Accelerated sustainable and inclusive growth rate

Abolition of Five Year Plans

- As India is a diverse and big, centralised planning could not work beyond a point due to its one-size-fits-all approach. Therefore, the Planning Commission was replaced by the NITI Aayog.
- Thus, there was no Thirteen Five Year Plan, however, the Five Year Defence Plan was made.
- The NITI Aayog have no financial role as they are only policy guide maps for the government.

15 Years Vision Document in Place of Five Year Plan

- The Five Years Plans were discontinued and were replaced with 15 Years Vision Document. The first 15 Year Vision Document came into effect from 2017-18 after the end of the Twelfth Five Year Plan.
- It was formulated with central objective of eradication of poverty. It came along-with a 7 year National Development Agenda which lay down the programmes, schemes and strategies to achieve a long term vision. The long vision document (Perspective plan) comprise three year mass economic framework :
  - 2017-18 to 2032-33 Vision Document
  - 2017-18 to 2024-25 National Development Agenda
  - 2017-18 to 2019-20 Three Year Action Agenda (to be repeated after every three year).

Extra Facts From Tamil Nadu Board and NIOS

- **Achievements of Economic Planning**
  1. Achievements in Economic Growth
  2. Creation of Infrastructure
  3. Development in Education
  4. Development of Science and Technology
  5. Expansion of Foreign Trade
- **Drawbacks of Planning**
  1. Failure to Remove Poverty and Inequality completely
  2. Problem of Unemployment Persists
  3. Failure to Curtail Corruption and Black Money
- NITI Aayog serves as a knowledge hub and monitors progress in the implementation of policies and programmes of the Government of India.

NITI Aayog is based on the 7 pillars of effective governance :

1. **Pro-People :** Fulfills the aspiration of society as well as individuals.
2. **Pro-Activity :** In anticipation and response to citizen needs.
3. **Participation :** Involvement of citizenry.
4. **Empowering :** Women in all respects.
5. **Inclusion of all :** SC, ST, OBC, minorities, gareeb, gaon, kishan.
6. **Equality :** Opportunity for the youth.
7. **Transparency :** Making government visible and responsive.

04

Poverty and Unemployment

[SOURCES]

Class-IX New NCERT Chap 2 (People as a Resource), Class-IX New NCERT Chap 3 (Poverty as a Challenge), Class-IX & X Old NCERT Chap 2 (An Overview of the Indian Economy), Class-X New NCERT Chap 2 (Sectors of the Indian Economy), Chap 1 (Development), Class XI New NCERT Chap 1 (Indian Economy on the Eve of Independence), Class XI New NCERT Chap 6 (Employment : Growth, Information and Other Issues), Chap 8 (Comparative Development Experiences of India and Its Neighbour)
Tamil Nadu Board (Class-XI), NIOS

Poverty

- Poverty is a state or condition in which a person or community lacks the financial resources and essentials for a minimum standard of living. Poverty means that the income level from employment is so low that basic human needs can't be met.
- Famous economist **Amartya Sen** had given the concept of poverty.
- According to him, monetary income plays an important role in eliminating poverty. As per him, poverty is the lack of capabilities.
- According to the **World Bank**, Poverty is pronounced deprivation in well-being and comprises many dimensions. It includes low incomes and the inability to acquire the basic goods and services necessary for survival with dignity.

Categories of Poor in India

There are various categories of poor in India depending on the incidence of poverty.

These are as follows :

- **Generational or Chronic Poor** This type of poverty is handed over to individuals and families from one generation to the next. Generally, people in this category are **Below Poverty Line** (BPL). E.g. landless farmers, casual labours, etc.
- **Churning Poor** They are the one who regularly move in and out of poverty.
- These are of two types
  - **Situational or Occasionally Poor** It is a temporary type of poverty based on occurrence of an adverse event like environmental disaster, job loss and severe health problem. People can help themselves even with a small assistance, as the poverty comes because of unfortunate events. (E.g. small farmers and seasonal workers).
  - **Transient Poor** Such poor are generally not poor. They fall in trap of poverty due to unfortunate event. E.g., gambler.
- **Never Poor** In this type, non-poor people are categorised whose income is higher than poverty line. E.g., businessmen, people employed in quaternary and quinary sector.
- **Rural Poor** They are found in non-metro areas with a population of fewer than 50,000 inhabitants. Due to the lesser population, the area lacks basic services and amenities which is the cause of their financial struggle.
- **Urban Poor** They are found in areas with a population of more than 50,000 inhabitants. These families live in much-stressed conditions due to overcrowding. They lack basic necessities like affordable housing.

Types of Poverty

There are two types of poverty i.e., Absolute poverty and Relative poverty.

Types of Poverty
- Absolute Poverty
- Relative Poverty

1. Absolute Poverty

- It is a condition where household income is below a necessary level to maintain basic living standards i.e., food, shelter, housing, etc. It was first introduced in 1990, the 'dollar a day' poverty line measured absolute poverty by the standards of the world's poorest countries.
- In October, 2015, the World Bank reset it to $1.90 a day.
- It was again updated in September, 2022 to US $ 2.15 per person per day.

2. Relative Poverty

- It refers to poverty on the basis of comparison of per capita income of different countries. It defined in comparison to other people's standing in the Economy. Thus a person who does not have a job and relies on Government assistance to mintain.

Poverty Line

- The incidence of poverty is measured by the poverty ratio, which is the ratio of the number of poor to the total population expressed as a percentage. It is also known as **head-count ratio.**
- Poverty line estimation in India is based on the consumption expenditure not on the income levels.
- The **World Bank** defines a person as extremely poor if she/he is living on less than $2.15 international dollars a day, which are adjusted for inflation as well as price differences between countries.
- **Asian Development Bank** (ADB) has its own poverty line; which is as of 2023, at $ 1.51 per person per day.

Inter-state Disparities of Poverty in India

- The distribution of poverty is not same throughout the country. Few states experience worse poverty conditions and few states have slightly less as compared to other states.
- The **National Multi-dimensional Poverty Index 2023** released by NITI Aayog, identifies 14.95% of India's population as multi-dimensionally poor.
- Between 2015-16 and 2019-21, around 13.5 crore people moved out of multi-dimensional poverty.
- Among Indian states, Bihar records the highest head-count poverty ratio with 33.76% of the population who are multi-dimensionally poor. It is followed by Jharkhand (28.81%), Meghalaya (27.79%), Uttar Pradesh (22.93%) and Madhya Pradesh (20.63%).
- The lowest head-count poverty ratio recorded in Kerala at 0.55%. It is followed by Goa (0.84%), Tamil Nadu (2.20%), Sikkim (2.60%) and Punjab (4.75%).
- Uttar Pradesh registered the highest decline in the number of poor with 3.43 crore, followed by Bihar and Madhya Pradesh. Improvement in nutrition, years of schooling, sanitation and cooking fuel played a significant role in bringing down poverty.

Poverty Estimation in India

- Poverty is measured based on consumer expenditure surveys of the **National Sample Survey Organisation** (NSSO). A poor household is defined as one with an expenditure level below a specific poverty line.
- Poverty estimation in India is carried out by NITI Aayog's task force through the calculation of poverty line based on the data captured by the National Sample Survey Office under the Ministry of Statistics and Programme Implementation (MoSPI).
- On the basis of consumption, there are two methods of poverty estimation :
  - **Uniform Recall Period** (URP) Here, consumption data is asked for a 30-days recall period for all items.
  - **Mixed Recall Period** (MRP) Here, consumption expenditure is asked for five infrequently used items i.e., clothing, footwear, durable goods, education and institutional medical expenses for a 365 days recall period and other items are asked for a 30-days recall period.

  Before independence, first time Dadabhai Naoroji estimated poverty in his book **'Poverty and Un-British Rule in India'**. In the year 1867-68, it was ₹ 16 to ₹ 35.
- **Planning Commission Expert Group** (1962) is a working group constituted by the Planning Commission formulated the separate poverty lines for rural and urban areas (₹ 20 and ₹ 25 per capita per year respectively).
- **VM Dandekar and N Rath** (1971) is known for the first systematic assessment of poverty in India, based on National Sample Survey (NSS) data. VM Dandekar and N Rath had the view that poverty line must be derived from the expenditure that was adequate to provide 2,250 calories per day in both rural and urban areas.
- **YK Alagh Committee** (1979) determined a poverty line based on a minimum daily requirement of 2,400 and 2,100 calories for an adult in rural and urban areas respectively.

International Standard of Poverty Estimation

At world level, **United Nation Development Programme** (UNDP) sets parameters to measure poverty, whereas, in India, NITI Aayog on the recommendations of committees, sets the parameters to measure poverty. Earlier, UNDP had set **Human Poverty** Index (HPI) as a parameter to measure poverty in its Human Development Reports, but 2010 onwards it switched over to a new parameter, namely, Multi-dimensional Poverty Index (MPI). Lorenz Curve and Gini Coefficient are the two international methods of poverty estimation.

1. Lorenz Curve

- It measures the income disparity between countries. It is developed by **Max O Lorenz** in the year 1905.
- The Lorenz Curve is used to represent economic inequality as well as unequal wealth distribution.
- The line at the 45° angle shows perfectly equal income distribution, while the other line shows the actual distribution of income.
- The further away from the diagonal, the more unequal the size of the distribution of income.
- Lorenz Curve of Income Distribution is given as follows:

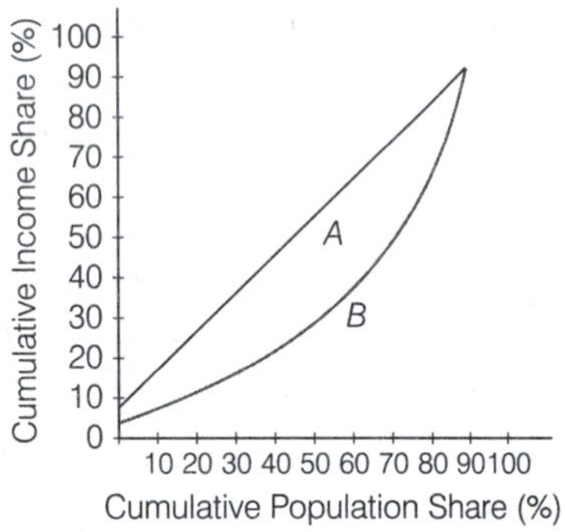

2. Gini Coefficient

- It was developed by Italian statistician **Carrado Gini** in 1912.
- It is a measure of inequality of income distribution. It is defined as a ratio with values between 0 and 1.
- Gini Coefficient of 1 (100 on percentile scale) expresses maximum inequality and zero shows minimum inequality.
- According to UNDP, Global Gini Coefficient Rate is 0.66. India's Gini Coefficient is around 0.34.
- The Gini Coefficient is usually defined mathematically based on the Lorenz Curve, which plots the proportion of the total income of the population (y axis) that is cumulatively earned by the bottom x% of the population.
- The line at 45° degrees Gini, thus, represents perfect equality of incomes.

$$\text{Gini Coefficient} = \frac{A}{A + B}$$

Where,

A = Area above Lorenz Curve

B = Area below Lorenz Curve

Inequality Adjustment

- **Amartya Sen** through his capability approach, credited to the creation of the Human Development Index (HDI), a composite measure of life expectancy and per capita income.
- The capability approach is an economic theory conceived as welfare economics.
- According to him, human development only can progress, if per capita income of all people gets increase simultaneously.
- Once there is increase in per capita income and visible decrease in income inequality, then there shall be increment in human development.

$$W = \mu\,(1\text{-}G)$$

Where, W = Welfare

μ = Per Capita Income

G = Age of Inequality

Committees Associated with Poverty Estimation in India

There are various committees which were formed to estimate the poverty level in India. These are discussed as follows :

Lakdawala Committee

- It was constituted in 1993 by the Planning Commission to consider methodological and computational aspects of estimation of proportion and number of poor in India. The report of this committee was submitted in July, 1993.
- It suggested that the consumption expenditure should be calculated based on calorie consumption as earlier.
- It also suggested that state specific poverty lines should be constructed and these should be updated using Consumer Price Index (CPI) – Industrial workers in urban areas and Agricultural labour in rural areas.

Tendulkar Committee Report

- Tendulkar Committee was headed by Mr. Suresh Tendulkar. This committee was formed in 2005 to look into the methodology of estimating poverty in India .
- Using this approach, new poverty line for the year 2004-05, has been raised from ₹ 356 per capita per month to ₹ 447 per capita per month in rural areas and from ₹ 539 per capita per month to ₹ 579 per capita per month in urban areas. In daily terms, poverty line has been raised from ₹ 12 to ₹15 per capita per day in rural areas and from ₹ 18 per capita per day to ₹ 19 per capita per day in urban areas.

- The new, updated data released by the commission based on the price indices computed from the 66th Round NSS 2009-10 data on Household Consumer Expenditure Survey, say anyone who has ₹ 28 to spend daily is out of poverty.
- It has estimated the poverty lines at all India level as MPCE (Monthly Per-Capita Consumption Expenditure) of ₹ 1000 for rural areas and ₹ 860 for urban areas in 2009-10.

SR Hashim Committee

- The Planning Commission had constituted an expert group 'Measurement of Poverty' UNDP under the Chairmanship of SR Hashim on 13th May, 2010.
- It recommend detailed methodology for identification of BPL families in urban areas in the context of the 12th Five Year Plan.
- The panel has suggested that the government should use a three-stage approach—automatic exclusion, automatic inclusion and scoring index to identify urban poor.

Rangarajan Committee

- Planning Commission in June, 2012 had constituted and expert group under the Chairmanship of Dr. C Rangarajan to review the methodology for measurement of poverty in the country.
- It had submitted its report on 30th June, 2014.
- The report retained consumption expenditure estimates of NSSO as the basis for determining poverty.
- On the basis of this, it pegged the total number of poor in India at 363 million or 29.6% of the population.
- This is higher than 269.8 million poor people or 21.9% pegged by the Suresh Tendulkar Committee.

Status of Poverty in India

- There is substantial decline in poverty ratios in India from about 45% in 1993-94 to about 21.9% in 2011-12.
- India lifted 271 million people out of poverty between 2006 and 2016. If the trend continues, people Below Poverty Line (BPL) may come down to less than 20% in the next few years.
- In a given year in India, official poverty lines finds higher in some states than in others because price levels vary from state-to-state.

Causes of Poverty in India

The following are the major causes of poverty in India:

Causes of Poverty in India

- Population Explosion
- Low Agricultural Productivity
- Inefficient Resource Utilisation
- Low Rate of Economic Development
- Price Rise
- Unemployment
- Lack of Capital and Entrepreneurship
- Social Facters
- Colonial Exploitation
- Climatic Factor
- Poverty Trap

- **Population Explosion** India's population has steadily increased through the years. During the past 45 years, it has risen at a rate of 2.2% per year, which means, on average, about 17 million people are added to the country's population each year. This also increases the demand for consumption goods tremendously.
- **Low Agricultural Productivity** A major reason for poverty is the low productivity in the agriculture sector. The reason for low productivity is manifold. Mainly, it is because of fragmented and subdivided land holdings, lack of capital, illiteracy about new technologies in farming, the use of traditional methods of cultivation, wastage during storage, etc.
- **Inefficient Resource Utilisation** There is under employment and disguised unemployment in the country, particularly in the farming sector. This has resulted in low agricultural output and also led to a dip in the standard of living.
- **Low Rate of Economic Development** Economic development has been low in India especially in the first 40 years of independence before the LPG reforms in 1991.
- **Price Rise** It has been steady in the country and this has added to the burden, the poor carry. Although, a few people have benefitted from this, the lower income groups have suffered because of it as they are not even able to satisfy their basic minimum needs.
- **Unemployment** It is another factor causing poverty in India. The ever-increasing population has led to a higher number of job-seekers. However, there is not enough expansion in opportunities to match this demand for jobs.
- **Lack of Capital and Entrepreneurship** The shortage of capital and entrepreneurship results in low level of investment and job creation in the economy.

- **Social Factors** Apart from economic factors, there are also social factors hindering the eradication of poverty in India. Some of the hindrances in this regard are the laws of inheritance, caste system, certain traditions, etc.
- **Colonial Exploitation** The British colonisation and rule over India for about two centuries, de-industrialised India by ruining its traditional handicrafts and textile industries. Colonial policies transformed India to a mere raw-material producers for European industries.
- **Climatic Factors** Most of India's poor belong to the states of Bihar, Uttar Pradesh, Madhya Pradesh, Chhattisgarh, Odisha, Jharkhand, etc. Natural calamities such as frequent floods, disasters, earthquakes and cyclones cause heavy damage to agriculture in these states.
- **Poverty Trap** It is a spiraling mechanism, which forces people to remain poor. It is so binding in itself that it doesn't allow the poor people to escape it. Poverty trap generally happens in developing and under-developing countries. It is caused by a lack of capital and credit to people.

Measures to Eradicate Poverty

The suggestive measures to eradicate poverty are as follows:

Measures to Eradicate Poverty

- Population Control
- Increase in Employment
- Stability in the Price Level
- Public Distribution
- Development of Agriculture
- Fulfilment of Needs
- Increase in the Productivity of Poor
- Increase in the Rate of Growth

- **Population Control** Population in India has been increasing rapidly. Growth rate of the population is very alarming. For removal of poverty, the growth rate of the population should be controlled.
- **Increase in Employment** Special measures should be taken to solve the problems of unemployment and disguised unemployment.
- Agriculture should be developed. Small scale and cottage industries should be developed in rural areas to generate employment.
- **Public of Distribution** The Public Distribution System (PDS) should be strengthened to remove poverty. Poor section should get food grains at subsidised rates and in ample quantities.
- **Fulfillment of Minimum needs of the Poor** Government should take suitable steps to meet minimum needs of the poor e.g., supply of drinking water and provision of primary health centres and primary education.
- **Increase in the Productivity of the Poor** To remove poverty, it is necessary to increase productivity of the poor. The poor should be given more employment. More investment should be made in public and private sectors to generate employment.
- **Stability in Price Level** Stability in prices helps to remove poverty. If prices continue to rise, the poor will become more poor.
- **Development of Agriculture** Agriculture should be developed as rapid rate of growth of agriculture production will help to remove urban as well as rural poverty. Agriculture should be mechanised/ modernised and marginal farmers should be given financial assistance.
- **Increase in the Rate of Growth** Slow rate of growth is the main cause of poverty. So, the growth rate must be accelerated by taking needful measures.

Unemployment

Unemployment occurs when a person, who is actively searching for employment is unable to find work. Unemployment is often used as a measure of the health of the economy. The most frequent measure of unemployment is the unemployment rate, which is the number of unemployed people divided by the number of people in the labour force.

National Sample Survey Organisation (NSSO) defines employment and unemployment on the following activity status of an individual:

- Working (engaged in an economic activity) i.e. 'Employed'.
- Seeking or available for work i.e. 'Unemployed'.
- Neither seeking nor available for work.

The first two constitute the labour force and the unemployment rate is the percentage of the labour force that is without work.

Unemployment Rate = (Unemployed workers/ Total labour force) × 100

Types of Unemployment

Various types of unemployment are categorised as:

Rural Unemployment

In rural areas of India, disguised unemployment and seasonal unemployment prevail. There description is given below:

Disguised Unemployment

- It is a situation, in which more persons are employed to do a job which can be done with equal efficiency by a less number of workers.

- The features of disguised unemployment are as follows:
  - Marginal productivity of labour is zero. However, Professor Sen does not agree with this view.
  - It is not possible to identify the persons who are actually unemployed.
  - Excess of population and lack of capital is the principal cause.
- Generally, it is associated with agricultural families.

Seasonal Unemployment

It is an unemployment that occurs during certain seasons of the year. Agricultural labourers in India rarely have work throughout the year.

Urban Unemployment

Urban Unemployment of India, is divided into two categories as :

- Educated Unemployment
- Industrial and Technological Unemployment

Educated Unemployment

- It refers to unemployment of those who are normally educated.
- This type of unemployment can be open unemployment and under employment type, i.e., those who can't find work and those who work in a job that is not in keeping with their skills, education or capacity.

Industrial and Technological Unemployment

- It is the loss of jobs due to changes in technology in industries. In 2016, World Bank data predicted that the proportion of jobs threatened by automation in India is 69% year-on-year. Technology has always displaced some work and jobs. In 1930, the economist John Maynard Keynes warned of a new disease that he termed as Technological unemployment.
- Technological unemployment is associated with technical changes. Modern industries are capital intensive and workers are being replaced by machines. Adoption of labour saving technologies renders some workers unemployed.

Unemployment in Both Rural and Urban Areas

- **Voluntary Unemployment** It occurs when a person is not willing to work at the prevailing rate of wage or does not desire to work. It is not taken into consideration while measuring unemployment in an economy.
- **Involuntary Unemployment** It is the situation, in which the worker is willing and able to work, but he does not get work. It is also called open unemployment.
- **Underemployment** It is situation, in which a person is engaged in economic activity but fails to provide him fully in accordance with his qualification and efforts.
- Thus, a person is employed but not in the desired capacity whether in terms of compensation hours or level of skill and experience.
- **Structural Unemployment** It is a category of unemployment arising from the mismatch between the jobs available in the market and the skills of the available workers in the market.
- Many people in India do not get jobs due to lack of requisite skills and due to poor education level, it becomes difficult to train them.
- **Cyclical Unemployment** It is the result of the business cycle, where unemployment rises during recessions and declines with economic growth. Cyclical unemployment figures in India are negligible. It is a phenomenon that is mostly found in capitalist economies.
- **Frictional Unemployment** It refers to the time lag between the jobs when an individual is searching for a new job or is switching between the jobs. In other words, an employee requires time for searching a new job or shifting from the existing to a new job, this inevitable time delay causes frictional unemployment. It is also called as Search unemployment. It is often considered as voluntary unemployment because it is not caused due to the shortage of jobs, but in fact, the workers themselves quit their jobs in search of better opportunities.
- **Vulnerable Employment** This means, people working informally, without proper job contracts and thus without any legal protection. These persons are deemed 'unemployed' since records of their work are never maintained. It is one of the main types of unemployment in India.

Causes of Unemployment

The following are the main causes for unemployment in India :

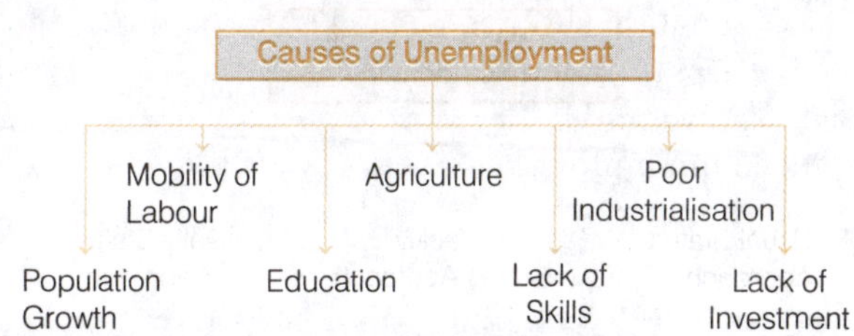

- **Population Growth** Rapid growth of population is the major reason for increasing unemployment in the country. In the last decade (2006-2016), India's population increased by 136 million and unemployment is at a Five year high in the financial year of 2015-2016. According to the latest 2022-23, Periodic Labour Force Survey (PLFS) the Unemployment Rate (UR) in India is 6.6%.

- **Mobility of Labour** Labour mobility is very low in India as because of their family loyalty, people generally avoid migrating to far-off areas of work. Factors like diversity of language, religion and customs also contribute to low mobility. Lower mobility causes greater unemployment.
- **Education** Although literacy rates have risen in the last few decades, there still remains a fundamental flaw in the education system in India. The curriculum is mostly theory-oriented and fails to provide vocational training required to match up with the current economic environment. The degree-oriented system fails when, it comes to producing human resources skilled enough to specific job profiles in the economy.
- **Agriculture** The problem of disguised unemployment is the biggest contributor behind this deficit. Also, the seasonal nature of employment in the sector leads to recurring cycles of unemployment for the rural population.
- **Lack of Skills** There has been a push towards providing employment opportunities to the people by the government by skilling them. But skill deficit still is a big issue.
- **Poor Industrialisation** The industrial sector in India still lag behind. Agriculture still remains as the biggest employer in the country.
- **Lack of Investment** Inadequacy of capital investment has been a key contributor in not generating enough industry that in turn provides employment to the labour force.

Measurement of Unemployment in India

National Sample Survey Office (NSSO), An organisation under Ministry of Statistics and Programme Implementation (MoSPI) measures unemployment in India on following approaches :

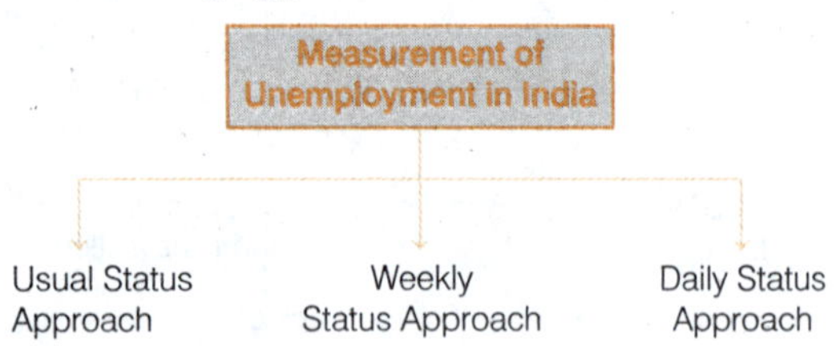

- **Usual Status Approach** This approach estimates only those persons as unemployed who had no gainful work for a major time during the 365 days preceding the date of survey.
- **Weekly Status Approach** This approach records only those persons as unemployed who did not have gainful work even for an hour on any day of the week preceding the date of survey.
- **Daily Status Approach** Under this approach, unemployment status of a person is measured for each day in a reference week. A person having no gainful work even for 1 hour in a day is described as unemployed for that day.

Impact of Unemployment in India

The following are the impacts of unemployment in India:

- The problem of unemployment gives rise to the problem of poverty. Young people after a long time of unemployment indulge in illegal activities for earning money which ultimately leads to an increase in crime.
- Unemployed persons can easily be persuaded by anti-social elements. This makes them lose faith in democratic values of the country.
- It is often seen that unemployed people end up getting addicted to drugs and alcohol or attempt suicide, leading losses to the human resources of the country.
- It also affects the economy of the country as the workforce that could have been gainfully employed to generate resources actually gets dependent on the remaining working population. Thus, escalating socio-economic costs for the state. For instance, 1% increase in unemployment reduces the GDP by 2%.

Government Programmes and Schemes Related to Poverty and Unemployment

The following are the few steps taken by the Government to tackle the menace of poverty and unemployment in India:

Support for Marginalised Individuals for Livelihood and Enterprise (SMILE)

- This scheme was launched in July, 2021. It includes Central Sector Scheme for comprehensive rehabilitation of persons engaged in the act of begging. This scheme focuses primarily upon, rehabilitation, provision of medical facilities, counselling, education and skill development of marginalised communities.

Atmanirbhar Bharat

- Prime Minister, Narendra Modi on 12th May, 2020 announced an economic stimulus package for ₹ 20-lakh crore (estimated at 10% of the GDP), towards building an Atmanirbhar Bharat or a self-reliant, resilient India. The Package is to cater to various sections including cottage industry, MSMEs, labourers, middle class and various indigenous industries. The aim is to make the country and its citizens independent and self-reliant in all senses.
- Five pillars of Atmanirbhar Bharat were outlined – Economy, Infrastructure, System, Vibrant Demography and Demand.

Pradhan Mantri Garib Kalyan Ann Yojana (PMGKAY)

- It is a part of Pradhan Mantri Garib Kalyan Package (PMGKP) launched on 26th March, 2020 to help the poor fight the battle against COVID-19. Its nodal Ministry is the Ministry of Finance.
- The scheme is aimed at providing each person, who is covered under the National Food Security Act, 2013 with an additional 5 kg grains (wheat or rice) for free, in addition to the 5 kg of subsidised foodgrain already provided through the Public Distribution System (PDS).

PM Svanidhi Yojana

- The Prime Minister Street Vendor's Atmanirbhar Nidhi (PM Svanidhi) was launched by the Ministry of Housing and Urban Affairs on 1st June, 2020 as a Central Sector Scheme with the following objectives:
  - To facilitate working capital loan upto ₹ 10,000.
  - To incentivise regular repayment, to reward digital transactions.
- The scheme will help formalise the street vendors across India who were severely hit by the COVID-19 pandemic as well as it will open up new opportunities to this sector to move up the economic ladder.

Atal Pension Yojana (APY)

- It was launched in the year 2015 to create a universal social security system for all Indians, especially the poor, the under-privileged and the workers in the unorganised sector. It is administered by Pension Fund Regulatory and Development Authority (PFRDA).
- The main objectives of the Atal Pension Yojana to provide security and protection to citizens in the scenarios like illness, accidents, diseases, etc. This scheme is mainly aimed at the unorganised sector in the country.

Pradhan Mantri Kaushal Vikas Yojana (PMKVY)

- It was launched in 2015 and has an objective of enabling a large number of Indian youth to take up industry-relevant skill training that will help them in securing a better livelihood.
- Ministry of Skill Development and Entrepreneurship (MSDE) has launched the updated Pradhan Mantri Kaushal Vikas Yojana (PMKVY) 3.0, in a bid to empower India's youth. It will be implemented in a more decentralised structure with greater responsibilities and support from states/Union Territories and districts.

Pradhan Mantri Jan Dhan Yojana (PMJDY)

- It is aimed at direct benefit transfer of subsidy, pension, insurance, etc and attained the target of opening 1.5 crore bank accounts. The scheme particularly targets the unbanked poor.
- It was launched on 28th August, 2014. It is a national mission with an aim to provide access to various financial services including Remittance, Credit, Insurance, Pension and Banking Savings in an affordable manner. The Accident Insurance Cover under Jan-Dhan Yojana of ₹ 1 lakh enhanced to ₹ 2 lakh to new PMJDY accounts opened after 28th August, 2018.

Extra Facts From Tamil Nadu Board and NIOS

- Peter Diamond, Dale Mortensen and Christopher Pissarides shared 2010 **Economics Nobel prize for jobs study**. Their model, called DMP model, helps us understand how regulation and economic policies affect unemployment, job vacancies and wages.
- **Vicious Circle of Poverty** Circular relationships that tend to perpetuate the low level of development in less developed countries. It operates both on demand side and supply side.
- According to the **Nurkse**, through the strategy of balanced growth, vicious circle of poverty operating on the demand side of capital formation can be broken.

Poverty Eradication Schemes

Schemes	Year of Launch
20 Point Programme (TPP)	1975
Food for Work Programme (FWP)	1977
Integrated Rural Development Programme(IRDP)	1978
Training Rural Youths for Self Employment (TRYSEM)	1979
National Rural Employment Programme (NREP)	1980
Rural Landless Employment Guarantee Programme(RLEGP)	1983
Jawahar Rozgar Yojana(JRY)	1989
Mahatma Gandhi National Rural Employment Guarantee Scheme (MGNREGS)	2006

- **Technical Unemployment** Modern technology being capital intensive requires less labourers and contributes to technological unemployment. Now a days, invention and innovations lead to the adoption of new techniques there by the existing workers are retrenched. Labour saving devices are responsible for technological unemployment.
- **Theories of Employment** Two theories propounded by economists regarding unemployment are
  1. **Classical Theory** According to the Say's Law of Market, "A person receives his income from production which is spent on the purchase of goods and services produced by others. For the economy as a whole, therefore, total production equals total income."
  2. **J. M. Keynes' Theory of Employment and Income** An increase in the aggregate effective demand would increase the level of employment. A decline in total effective demand would lead to unemployment. Therefore, total employment of a country can be determined with the help of total demand of a country.

05

Rural and Urban Development (Basic Infrastructure)

[SOURCES]

Class-IX & X Old NCERT Chap 3 (Infrastructure of Indian Economy), Class-XI New NCERT Chap 1 (Indian Economy on the Eve of Independence), Chap 5 (Rural Development)
Tamil Nadu Board (Class-XI), NIOS

Concept of Rural Development

- Rural development is the process of improving the quality of life and economic well-being of people living in rural areas, often relatively isolated and sparsely populated areas.
- Rural development has traditionally centered on the exploitation of land-intensive natural resources such as agriculture and forestry.
- Rural development still remains the core of the overall development of the country.
- More than two-third of the country's people are dependent on agriculture for their livelihood and one-third of rural India is still Below the Poverty Line (BPL).
- The objectives composed by the government for rural development are as follows:
  - To improve productivity and wages of rural people.
  - To guarantee increased and quick employment possibilities.
  - To demolish unemployment and bring a notable decline in underemployment.
  - To guarantee an increase in the standard of living of the underprivileged population.
  - To provide the basic needs i.e., elementary education, healthcare, clean drinking water, rural roads, etc.

Ministry of Rural Development

- In 1974, Department of Rural Development was established under Agricultural and Food Ministry.
- This department was formed as a Ministry of Rural Development on 20th January, 1980.
- The Ministry of Rural Development is a branch of the **Government of India** entrusted with the task of accelerating the socio-economic development of rural India. Its focus is on health, education, piped drinking water, public housing and roads.

Issues in Rural Development

The development of rural areas can be done only by solving the basic problems prevailing in these areas.

These problems can be classified as follows:

1. Rural Credit

- Growth of rural economy depends primarily on infusion of capital, from time to time, to realise higher productivity in agriculture and non-agriculture sectors.
- As the time gestation between crop sowing and realisation of income after production is quite long, farmers borrow credit from various sources to meet their initial investment on seeds, fertilisers, implements, etc.

Types of Rural Credit

Rural credit can be classified into the following categories:

- **Short-term credit** The Indian farmers require credit to meet their short-term needs viz., purchasing seeds, fertilisers, paying wages to hired workers, etc for a period of less than 15 months. Such loans are generally repaid after harvest.
- **Medium-term credit** This type of credit includes credit requirements of farmers for a medium period ranging between 15 months and 5 years and it is required for purchasing cattle, pumping sets, other agricultural implements, etc. Medium-term credits are normally larger in size than short-term credit.
- **Long-term credit** Farmers also require finance for a long period of more than 5 years just for the purpose of buying additional land or for making any permanent improvement on land like the sinking of wells, reclamation of land, horticulture, etc. Thus, the long-term credit requires sufficient time for the repayment of such loan.

Sources of Rural Credit

The sources of rural credit can be classified into two categories i.e., Institutional and Non-Institutional sources.

(i) Institutional Sources

Credit sources working under the formal system forms the Institutional sources. These are:

(a) Rural Cooperative Institutions

- Rural Cooperative Institutions are mandated to address the 'last mile problem' associated with the delivery of affordable credit to farmers.
- It can be broadly classified into **short-term** and **long-term** institutions, each with distinct mandates. The focus of short-term cooperatives, viz. State Cooperative Banks (SCBs), District Central Cooperative Banks (DCCBs), and Primary Agricultural Credit Societies (PACS) have been primarily providing crop loans and working capital loans to farmers and rural artisans.

(b) Commercial Banks

- In the initial period, the Commercial banks of our country have played a marginal role in advancing rural credit.
- In 1950-51, only 1% of the agricultural credit was advanced by the Commercial Banks.
- But after the nationalisation of Commercial Banks in 1969, the Commercial Banks started to extend financial support both directly and indirectly and also for both short and medium periods.
- With the help of 'Village Adoption Scheme' and Service Area approach, the Commercial Banks started to meet the credit and other requirements of the farmers.

(c) Regional Rural Banks (RRBs)

- RRBs are financial institutions that ensure adequate credit for agriculture and other rural sectors.
- Regional Rural Banks were set up on the basis of the recommend- ations of the Narasimham Working Group (1975) and after the legislation of the Regional Rural Banks Act, 1976.
- The equity of a Regional Rural Bank is held by the Central Government, concerned State Government and the Sponsor Bank in the proportion of 50:15:35.

> **National Bank for Agriculture and Rural Development (NABARD)**
>
> - **NABARD** is a development bank focussing primarily on the rural sector of the country. It is the apex banking institution to provide finance for agriculture and rural development.
> - Its headquarter is located in **Mumbai**, the country's financial capital. It is a statutory body established in 1982, under the Parliamentary Act- National Bank for Agriculture and Rural Development Act, 1981.
> - It was set up based on the **Shri B Sivaraman Committee recommendation.**
> - It provides refinance support for **building rural infrastructure.** It prepares district-level credit plans to guide and motivate the banking industry in achieving these targets.
> - It supervises Cooperative Banks and Regional Rural Banks (RRBs) and helps them develop sound banking practices and integrate them into the CBS (Core Banking Solution) platform.

(d) Self-Help Groups (SHGs)

- Self-Help Groups have emerged to fill the gap in the formal credit system because the formal credit delivery mechanism has not only proven inadequate.
- The SHGs promote good management in small proportions by a minimum contribution from each member.
- They pool money and credit is given to the needy members to be repayable in small installments at reasonable interest rates.
- In 2020, nearly 6 crore women in India have become member in 54 lakh women SHGs.
- About ₹ 10,000 - 15,000 per SHG and another ₹ 2.5 lakhs per SHG as a Community Investment Support Fund (CISF) are provided as part of renovating fund to take up self employment for income generation.
- Such credit provisions are generally referred to as **micro-credit programmes**. SHGs have helped in the empowerment of women.

(ii) Non-Institutional Sources

Non-Institutional sources of rural credit includes credit from moneylenders, traders and commission agents, relatives etc.

2. Rural Marketing

- Rural marketing comprises all operations involved in the movement of farm produce from the producer to the ultimate consumer.
- Issues (Problem faced) related with Rural marketing in India are as follows :
  - Too many middlemen
  - Lack of storage facilities in markets
  - Inadequate transportation facilities
  - Lack of institutional financing
  - Absence of grading and standardisation
  - Absence of market information
  - Unregulated local markets
  - Adulteration of commercial crops

3. Role of Cooperatives

- To work for similar objectives and profits is referred as **cooperative.**
- Cooperative societies under cooperative system are of two types :
  - **Credit Cooperative Society** It is a credit society that is a member-owned financial cooperative and controlled by its members. It provides loan at village level.
  - **Non-credit Cooperative Society** It is a society that works in the field of sugar production, wheat purchase, etc. These are formed in urban areas and provide loans to people living in urban or semi-urban areas.

4. Agricultural Diversification into Productive Activities

Agricultural diversification includes two aspects :

(i) Change in Cropping Pattern

- Diversification towards new areas is necessary not only to reduce the risk from agriculture sector but also to provide productive sustainable livelihood options to rural people.
- Most of the agricultural employment activities are concentrated in the Kharif season.
- During the Rabi season, in areas where there are inadequate irrigation facilities, it becomes difficult to find gainful employment.

(ii) Shift of Workforce from Agriculture to Other Allied Activities

- Expansion into other sectors is essential to provide supplementary gainful employment and in realising higher levels of income for rural people to overcome poverty and other tribulations.
- There is a need to focus on allied activities, non-farm employment and other emerging alternatives of livelihood, though there are many other options available for providing sustainable livelihoods in rural areas.

5. Sustainability and Organic Farming

- Traditional Indian agriculture was entirely based on the use of chemical fertilisers and pesticides. These chemicals enter in our food chain and create toxic effects on living beings.
- Soil quality also degrades due to use of chemicals in agricultural practices. Due to all these drawbacks, concept of sustainability and organic farming is given importance.
- Organic farming is a system which lays emphasis on ecological balance, conservation and protection.
- It is based on cheap inputs rather than costlier ones. Due to this, cost of investment in agriculture is less and profit is more.
- In world market, products of organic farming are in high demand. That's why, their export is a profitable business.
- In comparison to the food products produced from chemical fertilisers, food products of organic farming are more nutritious.

Rural Development and Panchayati Raj

- Panchayati Raj Institutions play an important role in rural development and that is why they have been given a constitutional status by the **73rd Amendment Act of 1992.**
- **Panchayati Raj Institutions** are involved in rural development through their participation in planning and execution at the village level.
- **Gram Sabha**, which is an integral part of the Panchayat system is being empowered to involve all the people in the decentralised planning.
- There have been **33% seats** reserved for women in all the three-tiers of Panchayati Raj Institutions.

e-Panchayat

- The main objective of e-Panchayat is to bring overall reform in the Panchayati Raj Institutions so as to make it more transparent, effective and accountable.
- In the **Twelfth Five Year Plan**, it was proposed to include e-Panchayat multimedia programmes in the Rajiv Gandhi Panchayat Empowerment initiative.

Rural Development Schemes

The following are the important rural development schemes of India :

SVAMITVA (Survey of Villages Abadi and Mapping with Improvised Technology in Village Areas)

- It is a new initiative of the Ministry of Panchayati Raj launched Nation-wide on 24th April, 2021.
- It aims to provide rural people with the right to document their residential properties so that, they can use their property for economic purposes.
- The scheme is for surveying the land parcels in rural inhabited areas using drone technology.
- The survey shall be done across the country in a phase wise manner over the period 2020-2025.
- The scheme is proposed as a Central Sector Scheme with a projected outlay of ₹ 79.65 crores for the pilot phase (Financial Year 2020 -21).

> **Jal Jeevan Mission**
> - This mission was launched on 15th August, 2019 to provide safe and adequate drinking water through individual household tap connection by 2024 to all households in rural India.
> - This mission comes under Jal Shakti Ministry. This ministry was formed in 2019 by merger of Ministry of Water Resources, River Development and Ministry of Drinking Water and Sanitation.

Gram Swaraj Abhiyaan

- Gram Swaraj Abhiyaan is a campaign that is being organised on the occasion of Ambedkar Jayanti between 14th April to 5th May, 2018.
- The campaign is undertaken under the name of "Sabka Sath, Sabka Gaon, Sabka Vikas".
- The objective of the campaign is to promote social harmony, spread awareness about pro-poor initiatives of government, reach out to poor households to enroll them as also to obtain their feedback on various welfare programmes.

Pradhan Mantri Awaas Yojana – Gramin

- It was launched to achieve the objective of **Housing for All by 2022**, the erstwhile rural housing scheme Indira Awaas Yojana (IAY) was restructured to Pradhan Mantri Awaas Yojana-Gramin (PMAY-G) on 1st April, 2016.
- Its objective is to help rural people Below the Poverty Line (BPL) in construction of dwelling units and upgradation of existing unserviceable kutcha houses by providing assistance in the form of a full grant.
- Its beneficiaries include people belonging to SCs/STs, freed bonded labourers and non-SC/ST categories, widows or next-of-kin of defence personnel killed in action, ex-servicemen and retired members of the Paramilitary forces, disabled persons and minorities.
- Beneficiaries are chosen according to data taken from the **Socio-Economic Caste Census** (SECC) of 2011.

Shyama Prasad Mukherjee Rurban Mission (SPMRM)

- PM Narendra Modi launched this scheme as National Rurban Mission on 21st February, 2016.
- This scheme was merged with Providing Urban Amenities in Rural Areas (PURA) Scheme.
- SPMRM is focused on comprehensive development of 300 Rurban clusters spread across the country.
- These clusters are identified in rural regions displaying potential for economic growth through the presence of thematic livelihood activities, increasing population and non-farm employment.
- The mission is being implemented with an aim to transform these clusters by focusing on developing skills, strengthening economic activities and provision of crucial basic infrastructure amenities in an equitable and time-bound manner.
- The benefits of Rurban mission are as follows :
  - Under this scheme, the facilities of cities will be given to villages. Electricity, water, roads and health facilities will be provided to villages.
  - The villages will be developed on the line of the cluster.
  - Population in a cluster will be 21,000 to 50,000.

Saansad Adarsh Gram Yojana (SAGY)

- It was launched in 2014, with the objective of creating **Adarsh Grams** across the country.
- In its first phase 2014-19, the scheme called upon the Members of Parliament (MPs) to make one Gram Panchayat of their choice, a Model Village by 2016 and another two by 2019.
- From 2019, under the second phase of the scheme, each Member of Parliament during his/her tenure may develop five model villages (one per year) in his/her area till 2024.

Deen Dayal Antyodaya Yojana – National Rural Livelihoods Mission (DAY-NRLM)

- It is a centrally sponsored programme, launched by the Ministry of Rural Development in June 2011.
- Its objective is to eliminate rural poverty through the promotion of multiple livelihoods and improved access to financial services for the rural poor households across the country.
- It involves working with community institutions through community professionals in the spirit of self-help, which is a unique proposition of DAY-NRLM.

Deen Dayal Upadhyaya Grameen Kaushalya Yojana

- It was launched in 2011. It is a placement linked skill Development Programme for Wage Employment.
- Skill development through Rural Self-Employment and Training Institutes (RSETIs) enables a trainee to take bank credit and start his/her own micro-enterprise. Some such trainees may also seek regular salaried jobs.
- At present, RSETIs offer training in 61 vocations classified under four major areas *viz.* agriculture, processing, product manufacture and general entrepreneurship development programme.

Providing Urban Amenities in Rural Areas (PURA)

- It is a strategy of rural development given by APJ Abdul Kalam. His vision was to develop rural India through a cluster development system where 50-100 villages with common competencies and/or mutual markets could be horizontally or vertically integrated as PURA complexes.
- These villages would be linked through 'four connectivities' i.e., physical, electronic, knowledge and economic.
- The scheme was approved by Government of India in January, 2004.

National Rural Drinking Water Programme (NRDWP)

- It was launched in 2009. It aims to provide safe and adequate water for drinking, cooking and other domestic needs to every rural person on a sustainable basis.
- It aimed to provide all rural habitations, government schools and anganwadis access to safe drinking water.

Pradhan Mantri Adarsh Gram Yojana (PMAGY) Rural

- It is a rural development programme launched by the Central Government in India in the Financial Year 2009-10.
- The aim of this programme is to development of villages having a higher ratio (over 50%) of people belonging to the Scheduled Castes (SCs) through convergence of central and state schemes and allocating financial funding on a per village basis.
- The scheme targets to make an 'Adarsh Gram' (Model village) that consists of sufficient physical and institutional infrastructure, with fully meeting the minimum requirements of every sector of the public.

Mahatma Gandhi National Rural Employment Guarantee Act (MGNREGA) 2005

- The scheme was introduced as a social measure that guarantees 'the right to work'. The Ministry of Rural Development monitors the entire implementation of this scheme in association with State Governments.
- Its major objective is providing not less than one hundred days of unskilled manual work as a guaranteed employment in a financial year to every household in rural areas as per demand, resulting in creation of productive assets of prescribed quality and durability.
- It is the Gram Sabha and the Gram Panchayat, which approves the self of works under MGNREGA and fixes their priority.
- Social audit of MGNREGA works is mandatory, which leads to accountability and transparency.

Pradhan Mantri Gram Sadak Yojana (PMGSY)

- It was launched on 25th December, 2000.
- Its objective is to provide connectivity, by way of an all-weather road to unconnected habitations.
- Its beneficiaries include unconnected habitations of designated population size (500+ in plain areas and 250+ in North-Eastern States, Himalayan States, Deserts and Tribal Areas as per 2001 census).

National Social Assistance Programme (NSAP)

- It was launched in 1995.
- It is targeted at any such person who has little or no regular means of subsistence from his/her own source of income or financial support from family members or other sources, to be identified by states/union Territories.
- At present, NSAP includes five sub-schemes as its components :
  - (i) Indira Gandhi National Old Age Pension Scheme
  - (ii) Indira Gandhi National Widow Pension Scheme
  - (iii) Indira Gandhi National Disability Pension Scheme (IGNDPS)
  - (iv) National Family Benefit Scheme
  - (v) Annapurna Scheme

Urban Development

Urban development is the social, cultural, economic and physical development of cities, and the underlying causes of these processes.

Urban Areas

Urban areas have been recognised as 'engines of inclusive economic growth'. Of the 121 crore Indians, 83.3 crore live in rural areas while 37.7 crore stay in urban areas, i.e., approx 32% of the population.

The Census of India, 2011 defines urban settlement as :

- **Statutory Towns** All the places, which have Municipality Corporation, Cantonment Board or notified town area committee. These towns are notified under law by respective state/Union

Territories, governments and have local bodies like Municipal Corporation, Municipality, etc, irrespective of demographic characteristics. For example- Vadodara (Municipal Corporation), Shimla (Municipal Corporation).

- **Census Town** All the other places, which satisfy following criteria :
  - A minimum population of 5,000 persons
  - At least 75 % of male main working population engaged in non-agricultural pursuits
  - A density of population of at least 400 persons per square kilometre

Note *These were identified on the basis of Census 2001 data. Cities are urban areas with more than 1,00,000 population. Urban areas below 1,00,000 are called towns in India.*

Urbanisation

- The process of urbanisation refers to a societal transformation taking place with the increased mobility and settling of people in urban surroundings.
- It is a process of geographic transformation with the perception of a better quality of life that includes better employment, education, healthcare, transportation, communication, housing, entertainment, etc.

Challenges Associated with Urbanisation in India

The following are the issues challenges with urbanisation in India :

- **Excessive Population Pressure** The cities suffer from the problems of slums, crime, unemployment, urban poverty, pollution, congestion, ill-health and several deviant social activities due to rural-urban migration.
- **Overflowing Slums** There are about 13.7 million slum households in the country sheltering a population of 65.49 million people across the country. As much as 65% of Indian cities have adjoining slums where people live in small houses adjacent to each other.
- **Inadequate Housing** Among the numerous social problems of urbanisation, the problem of housing is the most distressing. A vast majority of urban population live under conditions of poor shelter and in highly congested spaces.
- **Unplanned Development** The model of building a developed city comprises unplanned development, which only promotes difference prevailing in urban cities between the rich and the poor.
- **Pandemic-Induced Problems** The COVID-19 pandemic has exacerbated the misery of urban poor or slum dwellers. The sudden implementation of complete COVID lockdown severely affected the ability of slum dwellers to earn their living.
- **Non-Inclusive Welfare Schemes** The benefits of welfare schemes for urban poor often reach only a small part of the intended beneficiaries. Most relief funds and benefits do not reach slum dwellers, mainly because these settlements are not officially recognised by the government.

Urban Development Schemes

The following are the important urban development schemes of India :

Smart Cities Mission

- It was launched on 25th June, 2015.
- The main objective of the Mission is to promote cities by providing core infrastructure, clean and sustainable environment and give a decent quality of life to their citizens through the application of 'smart solutions'.
- The mission aims to drive economic growth and improve quality of life through comprehensive work on social, economic, physical and institutional pillars of the city.
- The focus is on sustainable and inclusive development by creation of replicable models, which act as lighthouses to other aspiring cities.
- 100 cities have been selected to be developed as Smart Cities through a two-stage competition.

Atal Mission for Rejuvenation and Urban Transformation (AMRUT)

- Jawaharlal Nehru National Urban Renewal Mission was renamed to Atal Mission for Rejuvenation and Urban Transformation (AMRUT) and then relaunched in June 2015.
- The focus is to establish infrastructure that could ensure adequate robust sewage networks and water supply for urban transformation by implementing urban revival projects.
- Rajasthan was the first state in the country to submit the State Annual Action Plan under Atal Mission for Rejuvenation and Urban Transformation (AMRUT).
- The components of the AMRUT consist of capacity building, reform implementation, water supply, sewerage and septage management, storm water drainage, urban transport and development of green spaces and parks.
- During the process of planning, the Urban Local Bodies (ULBs) will strive to include some smart features in the physical infrastructure components.

HRIDAY

- The National Heritage City Development and Augmentation Yojana (HRIDAY), a central sector scheme of the Government of India, was launched on 21st January, 2015.

- The main aim is bringing together urban planning, economic growth and heritage conservation in an inclusive manner and with the objective of preserving the heritage character of the city.
- Under the Scheme, twelve cities namely, Ajmer, Amritsar, Amaravati, Badami, Dwarka, Gaya, Kanchipuram, Mathura, Puri, Varanasi, Velankanni, Warangal have been identified for development.

Pradhan Mantri Awaas Yojana-Housing for All (Urban)

- The Mission is being implemented during 2015-2022* (now extended upto December 2024) and provides central assistance to Urban Local Bodies (ULBs) and other implementing agencies through states/ Union Terrritories for
  - In-situ Rehabilitation of existing slum dwellers using land as a resource through private participation Credit Linked Subsidy, Affordable Housing in Partnership Subsidy for beneficiary-led individual house construction/enhancement.
  - Credit linked subsidy component is being implemented as a Central Sector Scheme while other three components as Centrally Sponsored Scheme (CSS).
- All statutory towns as per Census 2011 and towns notified subsequently would be eligible for coverage under the Mission.

Swachh Bharat Mission-Urban

- The Swachh Bharat Mission - Urban (SBM-U), launched on 2nd October, 2014 aims at making urban India free from open defecation and achieving 100% scientific management of municipal solid waste in 4,041 statutory towns in the country.
- The objectives of the mission are :
  - Elimination of open defecation.
  - Eradication of Manual Scavenging.
  - Modern and Scientific Municipal Solid Waste Management.
  - To effect behavioural change regarding healthy sanitation practices.
  - Generate awareness about sanitation and its linkage with public health capacity augmentation for (Urban Local Bodies, ULBs).
  - To create an enabling environment for private sector participation in Capex (Capital expenditure) and Opex (Operation and maintenance expenditure).

National Urban Livelihoods Mission (NULM)

- It was launched by the Ministry of Housing and Urban Poverty Alleviation (MHUPA), Government of India on 23rd September, 2013 by replacing the existing Swarna Jayanti Shahari Rozgar Yojana (SJSRY).
- The NULM focuses on organising urban poor in their strong grassroots level institutions, creating opportunities for skill development leading to market-based employment and helping them to set up self-employment ventures by ensuring easy access to credit.
- It is aimed at providing shelter equipped with essential services to the urban homeless in a phased manner. In addition, it would also address livelihood concerns of the urban street vendors.

Other Schemes of Rural and Urban Development

Other government schemes related to the rural and urban development are as follows :

Ayushman Bharat Yojana

- It has been launched by the government on 23rd September, 2018 with an aim to move towards a provision of universal healthcare by providing insurance cover of ₹ 5 Lakh per family per year, taking care of almost all secondary care and tertiary care procedures.
- There is no limitation on family size and age to avail the scheme. It is a centrally sponsored health insurance scheme of Ministry of Health and Family Welfare (MOHFW).
- Ayushman Bharat adopts a two-way approach :
  - Firstly, the creation of health and wellness centres to bring health care closer to homes.
  - Secondly, the formulation of a Pradhan Mantri Jan Aarogya Yojana (PMJAY) to protect poor and vulnerable families against financial risk arising out of catastrophic health episodes.

Pradhan Mantri Suraksha Bima Yojana

- It is a government scheme launched on 9th May, 2015.
- It intends to provide an affordable insurance scheme for the poor and underprivileged people in the age group of 18 to 70 years with a bank account at a premium of ₹ 12 per annum.
- It provides a risk coverage of ₹ 2 lakh for accidental death and full disability and ₹ 1 lakh for partial disability.

Mission Indradhanush

- It was launched on 25th December, 2014. Its aim is to fully immunise more than 89 lakh children who are either unvaccinated or partially vaccinated under Universal Immunisation Programme (UIP).
- It targets children under 2 years of age and pregnant women for immunisation.
- It provides vaccination against 12 Vaccine-Preventable Diseases (VPD) i.e. diphtheria, whooping cough, tetanus, polio, tuberculosis, hepatitis B, meningitis and pneumonia, Haemophilus influenzae type B infections, Japanese Encephalitis (JE), rotavirus vaccine, Pneumococcal Conjugate Vaccine (PCV) and Measles-Rubella (MR).

List of the Some Major Rural and Urban Development Programmes

Name of the Programme	Year of Beginning	Objectives/Description
Gati Shakti Yojana	2021	To provide multi-modal connectivity for movement of people, goods and services from one mode of transport to another.
Atmanirbhar Bharat Rojgar Yojana	2020	To boost employment in formal sector during COVID phase.
Five Star Villages Scheme	2020	To ensure 100% rural coverage of postal product and services.
PM Svanidhi Scheme	2020	It is a special micro credit facility scheme for providing affordable loan to street vendor.
Pradhan Mantri Shram Yogi Maandhan Yojana	2019	To provide ₹ 3,000 per month to 60 year old unorganised sector worker.
Pradhan Mantri Kisan Mandhan Yojana	2019	To provide ₹ 3,000 per month as pension to farmers.
Rashtriya Poshan Yojana	2018	To improve nutritional outcomes for children, pregnant women and lactating mothers.
Pradhan Mantri Vaya Vandana Yojana	2017	Pension scheme for Senior Citizens (above 60 years of age)
Sahaj Bijli Har Ghar Yojana	2017	To provide electricity for all the household in rural and urban areas.
Pradhan Mantri Ujjwala Yojana (PMUY)	2016	To distribute LPG connections to women of Below Poverty Line (BPL) families.
Nirmal Bharat Abhiyan	2012	Total Sanitation Campaign (TSC) renamed to Nirmal Bharat Abhiyan. On 2nd October, 2014, the campaign was relaunched as Swachh Bharat Abhiyan (Clean India Mission).
Bal Bandhu Scheme	2011	Provides for protection of children in areas of civil unrest. It is implemented by NCPCR with grant from PM's National Relief Fund.
Rajiv Gandhi Scheme for Empowerment of Adolescent Girls (RGSEAG) 'Sabla'	2010	It aims at empowering adolescent girls of 11 to 18 years by improving their nutritional and health status. Upgradation of home skills and vocational skills.
Pradhan Mantri Swasthya Suraksha Yojana (PMSSY)	2010	To correct regional imbalance in tertiary healthcare and augmenting facilities for quality medical education in the country; and setting up six AIMS like institutions in Phase-1 and in Phase-2, two more AIIMS like institutions.
Integrated Child Protection Scheme (ICPS)	2009-10	Providing a safe and secure environment for comprehensive development of children who are in need of care and protection as well as children in conflict with law.
Saakshar Bharat	2009	National Literacy Mission has been recasted as 'Saakshar Bharat'. The aim is to cover all adults, the age group of 15 and above, with its primary focus on women.
Rashtriya Madhyamik Shiksha Abhiyan (RMSA) or Scheme for Universalisation of Access for Secondary Education (SUCCESS).	2009	To ensure universal access by 2017 and universal retention by 2020.
Rajiv Gandhi National Creche Scheme for the Children of Working Mothers	2006	Overall development of children, childhood protection, complete immunisation, awareness generation among parents of malnutritioned children, health and education.
Jawaharlal Nehru Urban Renewal Mission (JNURM). It has two components : (a) Basic Services to Urban-Poor, and (b) Integrated Housing and Slum Development Programme	2005	To assist cities and towns in taking up housing and infrastructural facilities for the urban poor in 63 cities (now 65 cities) in the country.
National Rural Health Mission (NRHM)	2005	It was launched to provide healthcare services to the rural population.
Nirmal Gram Puraskar (NGP)	2003	It is an incentive scheme to encourage Panchayati Raj Institutions (PRIs) to take up sanitation promotion. Sikkim has become the 1st Nirmal State in the country.
Swayam Siddha	2001	Organising women into **Self-Helf Groups** to form a strong institutional base.
Pradhan Mantri Gramodya Yojana (PMGY)	2000	Focus on village level development in 5 criticial areas i.e., primary health, primary education, housing, rural roads and drinking water and nutrition.

Extra Facts From
Tamil Nadu Board and NIOS

Self-Help Groups (SHGs)

It is generally an economically homogeneous group formed through a process of self-selection based upon the affinity of its members. SHGs are self-managed institutions characterised by participatory and collective decision-making.

06

Agriculture

[SOURCES]

Class-IX New NCERT Chap 1 (The Story of Village Palampur),
Chap 4 (Food Security in India), Class-X New NCERT Chap 3 (Money and Credit),
Class-IX & X Old NCERT Chap 4 (Towards Economic Development),
Class-XI New NCERT Chap 1 (Indian Economy on the Eve of Independence),
Chap 2 (Indian Economy (1950-1990),
Class-XI New NCERT Chap 5 (Rural Development)
Tamil Nadu Board (Class-XI), NIOS

Introduction to Indian Agriculture

- Agriculture is defined as the art, science and business of producing crops and livestock for economic purposes.
- Agriculture comes under the primary sector of the Indian economy.
- It plays an important role in the Indian economy as around 50% of the population is still dependent on agriculture and allied activities.
- This is the reason why India is known as an Agriculture-based economy.
- Agriculture sector includes core farming, horticulture, animal husbandry, dairy, fishing, etc.
- Agriculture is a dominant sector in India, contributing 19.9% to the total GDP (Gross Domestic Product). The increasing population of India is dependent on this sector for its living.

Reforms in Indian Agriculture

- The credit for systematic changes in Indian agriculture is given to the policies of land reforms and Green Revolution.
- In the era of 1951, first attempt was made to bring equality in agriculture with land reforms, with major aim of changing the ownership of the holdings. In addition to promote equality, importance was given to fixing the ceiling.
- It was majorly done to decrease the ownership of agriculture land of an individual with determining the maximum amount of ownership of agricultural land.
- At the time of independence, 75% of the country's population was dependent on agriculture.
- Due to low productivity and use of outdated technology, the farmers lacked proper infrastructure, this problem was replaced by introduction of Green Revolution in the country.

Significance of Agriculture in Indian Economy

The following points highlight significance of agriculture sector in Indian economy :

Contribution of Agriculture in National Income

- Agricultural sector contributes a significantly large share to the national income of India. The share of Gross Domestic Product (GDP) of agriculture and sector in total economy is 18.3% in FY 2022-23. The share of agriculture in GDP increased to 19.9% in 2021-21 from 17.8% in 2019-20.
- During the COVID-19 pandemic, it was the only sector to witness a positive growth rate. In 2020-21, the percentage share of Gross Value Added (GVA) of Agriculture and Allied sector to total economy reached 20.2%

Contribution of Agriculture in Employment

- The share of agriculture has been falling in the country's gross income while industrial and service sectors' shares have been on a rise constantly. But from the livelihood point of view, about 52% people of India depend on agricultural sector.
- In 2022-23, contribution of agriculture in GDP was 18.3% which increases exports and improves India's trade deficit.

Contribution in Economic Growth and Capital Formation

- Economic transformation in developing nations is propelled by increase in agricultural incomes and industrial growth. For example, China's economic growth.
- Agriculture has the potential to increase India's overall Gross Domestic Product (GDP) growth.
- There is general agreement on the necessity of capital formation. Since agriculture happens to be the largest industry in a developing country like India, it can and must play an important role in pushing up the rate of capital formation.

Contribution of Agriculture in Industries

- Agriculture supplies raw materials to various agro-based industries like sugar, jute, cotton textile and Vanaspati industries. Food processing industries are similarly dependent on agriculture. Therefore, the development of these industries entirely depends on agriculture.
- Increase in rural purchasing power is very necessary for industrial development as two-thirds of the Indian population live in villages. After the Green Revolution, the purchasing power of the large farmers increased due to their enhanced income and negligible tax burden.
- Indian agriculture plays a vital role in internal and external trade of the country. Internal trade in food grains and other agricultural products helps in the expansion of the service sector. In the year 1990-91, export share of Agriculture sector was 1.9% which increased to 2.46% in 2020-21. India has also rapidly emerged as the net exporter of agricultural products in recent years. With the agricultural exports touching US$ 50. 2 billion in FY 22-23.

Agricultural Inputs

Land is the most important input for the agriculture. Apart from land, following agricultural inputs are essential for agriculture :

- Technical knowledge
- Livestock
- Irrigation
- Fertilisers and insecticides
- Labour
- Agro-implements
- Seeds
- Storage

Salient Features of Indian Agriculture

The following are the salient features of Indian agriculture :

- **Dependence on Monsoon** Agriculture in India mainly depends on monsoon. If monsoon is good, the production will be more and if monsoon is less than average then the crops fail. Sometimes floods destroy the crops. As irrigation facilities are quite inadequate, agriculture depends on the monsoon.
- **Labour Intensive Cultivation** Due to the increase in population, the pressure on land holding increased. Land holdings get fragmented and subdivided and become uneconomical. Machinery and equipment cannot be used on such farms.
- **Under Employment** Due to inadequate irrigation facilities and uncertain rainfall, the production of agriculture is less, farmers find work a few months in the year. Their capacity of work cannot be properly utilised. In agriculture, there is under employment as well as disguised unemployment.
- **Small Size of Holdings** Due to large scale sub-division and fragmentation of holdings, land holding size is quite small.
- (Agriculture Census 2015-16) Average size of land holding was 1.08 hectares in India while in Australia it was 1993 hectares and in the USA it was 158 hectares.
- **Traditional Methods of Production** In India, methods of production of agriculture along with equipment are traditional. It is due to poverty and illiteracy of people. Traditional technology is the main cause of low production.
- **Low Agricultural Production** Agricultural production is low in India. India produces 27 Qtls wheat per hectare. France produces 71.2 Qtls per hectare and Britain 80 Qtls per hectare. Average annual productivity of an agricultural labourer is $ 162 in India, $ 973 in Norway and $ 2408 in USA.
- **Dominance of Food Crops** 75% of the cultivated area is under food crops like wheat, rice and bajra, while 25% of cultivated area is under commercial crops. This pattern is the cause of backwardness of agriculture.

Challenges Associated with India's Agriculture Sector

There are various challenges associated with Indian agriculture. Prominent among them are as follows :

Issues Related to Subsidies

- Agricultural subsidies were introduced to incentivise farmers to take up the Green Revolution. Subsidies also intended to reduce the cost of production for farmers and to check food price inflation and protect consumers.

- However, today it has become apparent that subsidies are inflicting significant damage on different aspects of the economy.
- Subsidised urea has led to massive overuse of nitrogenous fertilisers, leading to damaged soils and pollution of local water bodies.
- Similarly, power subsidies have not only led to an alarming overuse of groundwater, but also it has severely damaged the health of power distribution companies.
- Credit subsidies like loan waivers have weakened the Indian Banking System (due to increased NPAs), having negative spillover effects on the economy.
- Output price supports in the form of **Minimum Support Price** (MSP) basically apply to only a handful of crops, especially wheat and rice that are procured by the government in a handful of states.

Consumer Oriented Policies

- Whenever there is a price rise in any agricultural commodity, the government imposes restrictions on exports to protect Indian consumers. It creates hindrances for farmers taking advantage of high prices in foreign markets.
- High prices alongwith the Essential Commodities Act (ECA), has declined private investment in export infrastructure such as warehouses and cold storage systems. This lack of storage infrastructure compels farmers to go for distress sale.

Agriculture Marketing

- It includes the operations such as collecting, grading, processing, preserving, transportation and financing.
- The actors in product marketing include farmers, traders, wholesalers, processors, importers, exporters, marketing cooperatives, regulated market committees and retailers.

Various Marketing Methods

The various marketing methods are as follows :

- **Rural Primary Markets** Periodic markets or haats and fairs (melas, jatras) are the major rural markets in India. Rural primary markets include mainly the periodical markets known as *haats*, *shandies*, *painths* and *fairs*. The producers sell their produce directly to the consumers or to small rural retailers.
- **Cooperative Marketing** The cooperative marketing is an alternative to the private dealers with the main objective of securing a large share of profits for the producer.
- **Contract Farming** It can be defined as agricultural production carried out according to an agreement between a buyer and farmers, which establishes conditions for the production and marketing of a farm product or products. Typically, the farmer agrees to provide agreed quantities of a specific agricultural product.
- **Commodity Market** It is about trading of precious metals, energy, oil, spices and so on. There are three commodity markets in India i.e.,
  - National Commodity and Derivative Exchange.
  - Multi-Commodity Exchange.
  - National Multi-Commodity Exchange of India.
- **Future Market** In future contracts, the buyer has the obligation to purchase a specific assets and the seller has to sell and deliver that asset at a specific future date. Agri-futures markets are considered to be one of the ways to ensure appropriate farm prices.

Agricultural Marketing Policies

- Due to restrictions imposed by Agricultural Produce Market Committee (APMC) Acts passed by various states, Indian farmers can only sell their produce at farm gate or local market (*haat*) to village aggregators, APMC *mandis* and to the government at the Minimum Support Price (MSP).
- The introduction of the Electronic National Agriculture Market (e-NAM)—an online trading platform for agricultural commodities in India—is a step in the right direction. However, its effects have been underwhelming due to three major factors :
  - Time cost of transactions
  - Quality assessment challenges
  - Transportation logistics

Marginal Land Holdings

- Raising farm productivity is critical for long-term increase in farmers income in India, as land fragmentation means that many Indian farmers are farming plots of such small sizes that even doubling their incomes would leave them with meagre earnings.
- In India, nearly 85% of agricultural land holdings are small and marginal (less than 2 hectare).
- The **Ashok Dalwai Committee Report** on doubling farmers' income, estimated that doubling farmers' income will require an agricultural growth rate of 10-11% per annum, until 2022–23.
- However, agricultural growth rate and farmers' income growth rate has been stagnating and well below the required rate of growth.

Efforts of Government in the Field of Agriculture

Government has taken many steps to improve agriculture marketing. Some of these are :

- **Kisan Rail** They are multi commodity trains consisting of refrigerated coaches to swiftly transport perishable agricultural products from supply centres to demand centres.
- **Agricultural Produce Market Committee** (APMC) An APMC is a marketing board established by a State Government in India to ensure: farmers are safeguarded from exploitation by large retailers. They also ensure that the farm to retail price spread does not reach excessively high levels.
- **Agricultural Marketing Information Network** (AGMARKNET) The AGMARKNET is a G2C e-governance portal. It caters to the needs of various stakeholders such as farmers, industry, policy-makers and academic institutions by providing agricultural marketing related information from a single window.
- **e- NAM** National Agriculture Market (e-NAM) is pan-India electronic trading portal linking existing APMC mandis to create a unified national market for agricultural commodities.
- **Commodity Boards** Commodity Boards were set up to operate for rubber, coffee, tea, tobacco, spices, coconut, oilseed and vegetable oils, horticulture, etc. The National Dairy Development Board is also engaged in the marketing of agricultural commodities.
- **Soil Health Card Scheme** The scheme was launched by Government of India in February, 2015. Under this scheme, the government plans to issue soil cards to farmers which will carry crop-wise recommendations of nutrients and fertilisers required for the individual farmers to help farmers to improve productivity.
- **Agri-export Policy 2018** The government introduced the policy with the objectives- to strive to double India's share in world agri-exports by integrating with global value chains and enables farmers to get benefit of export opportunities in overseas market.
- **Pradhan Mantri Krishi Sinchayee Yojana** (PMKSY) PMKSY is a centrally sponsored scheme (Core Scheme) launched in 2015. Under the scheme, centre-states ratio will be 75:25%.
- In the case of the North-Eastern region and hilly states, this ratio will be 90:10%.
- **Kisan Urja Suraksha Evam Utthaan Mahabhiyan** (KUSUM) It aims to promote use of solar energy among the farmers. Installation of standalone off-grid solar water pumps to fulfil irrigation needs of farmers not connected to grid. Solarisation of existing grid-connected agriculture pumps to make farmers independent of grid supply and also sell surplus solar power generated to Discom and get extra income.
- **Meghdoot App** The Ministry of Earth Sciences and Agriculture have launched a mobile application that will provide location and crop or livestock-specific weather-based agro advisories to farmers in local languages. It has been developed by experts from the India Meteorological Department and Indian Institute of Tropical Meteorology and the Indian Council of Agricultural Research.
- **Kaleshwaram Lift Irrigation Project** The Kaleshwaram project is an off-shoot of the original Pranahita-Chevella Lift Irrigation Scheme taken up by the government in 2007 when Andhra Pradesh was not divided. It is aimed to make Telangana drought proof by harnessing the flood waters of the Godavari,

Organic Farming

- According to Food Safety and Standard Authority of India (FSSAI), "Organic farming is a system of farm design and management to create an ecosystem of agriculture production without the use of synthetic external inputs such as chemical fertilisers, pesticides and synthetic hormones or genetically modified organisms."
- Organic farm produce means the produce obtained from organic agriculture, while organic food means food products that have been produced in accordance with specified standards for organic production.

Indian Scenario Regarding Organic Farming

- Sikkim became the first state in the world to become fully organic in 2016.
- North-East India has traditionally been organic and the consumption of chemicals is far less than the rest of the country.
- Similarly, the tribal and island territories have been traditionally practicing organic farming. The major organic exports from India have been flax seeds, sesame, soyabean, tea, medicinal plants, rice and pulses.

Government Initiatives in the Field of Organic Farming

Government initiatives to promote organic farming are as follows :

- **Mission Organic Value Chain Development for North-East Region** (MOVCD) It is a Central Sector Scheme, a sub-mission under National Mission for Sustainable Agriculture (NMSA).

  It was launched by the Ministry of Agriculture and Farmers Welfare in 2015 for implementation in the States of Arunachal Pradesh, Assam, Manipur, Meghalaya, Mizoram, Nagaland, Sikkim and Tripura.

The scheme aims to develop certified organic production in a value chain mode to link growers with consumers and to support the development of the entire value chain.

- **Paramparagat Krishi Vikas Yojana** (PKVY) was launched in 2015 is an extended component of Soil Health Management (SHM) of the major project National Mission of Sustainable Agriculture (NMSA). under PKVY, Organic Farming is promoted through adoption of organic villages by cluster approach and Participatory Guarantee System (PGS) certification.
- **Certification Schemes** Food Safety and Standards Authority of India (FSSAI) is the food regulator in the country and is also responsible for regulating organic food in the domestic market and imports.
- **Participatory Guarantee System** (PGS) It is a process of certifying organic products, which ensures that their production takes place in accordance with laid-down quality standards. PGS green is given to chemical free produce under transition to 'organic' which takes 3 years. It is mainly for domestic purposes.
- **One District - One Product** (ODOP) The programme aims to encourage more visibility and sale of indigenous and specialised products/crafts of a particular region or district, generating employment at the district level. The presence of aggregators is imperative to bring about economies of scale for the small and marginal farmers.
- **PM Formalisation of Micro Food Processing Enterprises** (PM FME) The Ministry of Food Processing Industries (MoFPI) launched the PM FME scheme as a part of 'Atmanirbhar Bharat Abhiyan'. It aims to bring in new technology, apart from affordable credit to help small entrepreneurs penetrate new markets.
- **Zero Budget Natural Farming** It is a method of chemical-free agriculture drawing from traditional Indian practices.
- **National Programme for Organic Production** (NPoP) NPoP is managed by Agriculture and Processed Food Products Export Development Authority (APEDA) under the ministry of Commerce and Industry. NPoP provides standards for organic production, systems, criteria and procedure for accreditation of certification bodies.

Minimum Support Price (MSP)

- The MSP is the rate at which the government purchases crops from farmers, and is based on a calculation of at least one-and-a-half times the cost of production incurred by the farmers.
- MSP is a 'minimum price' for any crop that the government considers as remunerative for farmers and hence deserving of 'support'.
- The **Commission for Agricultural Costs and Prices** (CACP) recommends MSPs for 22 mandated crops and Fair and Remunerative Price (FRP) for sugarcane.
- CACP is an attached office of the Ministry of Agriculture and Farmers Welfare.
- The mandated crops include 14 crops of the kharif season, 6 rabi crops and 2 other commercial crops.
- In addition, the MSPs of toria and de-husked coconut are fixed on the basis of the MSPs of rapeseed/mustard and copra, respectively.
- The CACP considers various factors while recommending the MSP for a commodity, including cost of cultivation.
- It takes into account the supply and demand situation for the commodity, market price trends (domestic and global) and parity vis-a-vis other crops, and implications for consumers (inflation), environment (soil and water use) and terms of trade between agriculture and non-agriculture sectors.
- The **Cabinet Committee on Economic Affairs** (CCEA) of the Union Government takes a final decision on the level of MSPs and other recommendations made by CACP.

Government Steps for MSP

The following steps were taken by the Government of India for MSP :

- **Pradhan Mantri Annadata Aay Sanrakshan Abhiyan** (PM-AASHA) PM-AASHA was launched to ensure adequate prices to farm produce. It was launched in 2018. It had following three components:
  - Price Support Scheme (PSS)
  - Price Deficiency Payment Scheme (PDPS)
  - Private Procurement and Stockist Scheme (PPSS)
- **Pradhan Mantri Kisan Samman Nidhi** (PM-KISAN) Under the scheme, the Centre transfers an amount of ₹ 6,000 per year, in three equal installments, directly into the bank accounts of all landholding farmers irrespective of the size of their land holdings. It was launched in February 2019. It is a Central Sector Scheme with 100% funding from the Government of India.

  It is being implemented by the Ministry of Agriculture and Farmers Welfare. The entire responsibility of identification of beneficiary farmer families rests with the State / union Terrirory Governments.

Crop Insurance

- Crop insurance is to protect farmers against either the loss of their crops due to natural disasters, such as hail, drought and floods, or the loss of revenue due to declines in the prices of agricultural commodities.
- The scheme Pradhan Mantri Fasal Bima Yojana (PMFBY) was launched in 2016 and is being administered by the Ministry of Agriculture and Farmers Welfare.

- It replaced the National Agricultural Insurance Scheme (NAIS) and Modified National Agricultural Insurance Scheme (MNAIS).
- It aims to provide a comprehensive insurance cover against the failure of the crop thus helping in stabilising the income of the farmers.
- All food and oilseed crops and annual commercial/horticultural crops for which past yield data is available are covered.
- The prescribed premium is 2% to be paid by farmers for all kharif crops and 1.5% for all rabi crops. In the case of annual commercial and horticultural crops, the premium is 5%.

Food Security

- Food security, as defined by the United Nations' Committee on World Food Security, means that all people, at all times, have physical, social and economic access to sufficient, safe and nutritious food that meets their food preferences and dietary needs for an active and healthy life.
- Food security is the combination of the following three elements:
  - **Food Availability** i.e., food must be available in sufficient quantities and on a consistent basis. It considers stock and production in a given area and the capacity to bring in food from elsewhere, through trade or aid.
  - **Food Accessibility** i.e., people must be able to regularly acquire adequate quantities of food, through purchase, home production, barter, gifts, borrowing or food aid.
  - **Food Affordability** i.e., people must be able to afford food.

National Food Security Mission

- It is a centrally sponsored scheme launched in 2007.
- It aims to increase production of rice, wheat, pulses, coarse cereals and commercial crops, through area expansion and productivity enhancement.
- It works towards restoring soil fertility and productivity at the individual farm level and enhancing farm level economy.
- It further aims to augment the availability of vegetable oils and to reduce the import of edible oils.

National Food Security Act (NFSA), 2013

- It legally entitles up to 75% of the rural population and 50% of the urban population to receive subsidised food grains under the Targeted Public Distribution System.
- The eldest woman of the household of age 18 years or above is mandated to be the head of the household for the purpose of issuing ration cards under the act.

Public Distribution System (PDS)

- It is an Indian Food Security System established under the Ministry of Consumer Affairs, Food and Public Distribution.
- PDS evolved as a system of management of scarcity through distribution of food grains at affordable prices.
- PDS is operated under the joint responsibility of the Central and the State Governments.
- The Central Government, through Food Corporation of India (FCI), has assumed the responsibility for procurement, storage, transportation and bulk allocation of food grains to the State Governments.
- The operational responsibilities including allocation within the state, identification of eligible families, issue of ration cards and supervision of the functioning of Fair Price Shops (FPSs) etc., rest with the State Governments.
- Under the PDS, presently the commodities namely as wheat, rice, sugar and kerosene are being allocated to the states/union Territories for distribution. Some states/union Territories also distribute additional items of mass consumption through the PDS outlets such as pulses, edible oils, iodised salt, spices, etc.

Agriculture Allied Sector

Agriculture allied sector include livestock/animal rearing, fisheries sector horticulture, floriculture, etc.

Livestock/Animal Rearing

- Livestock is commonly defined as domesticated animals raised in an agricultural setting to produce labour and commodities such as meat, eggs, milk, fur, leather and wool.
- There are about 302.79 million bovines, 108.95 million buffaloes 74.26 million sheep, 148.88 million goats and about 9.06 million pigs as per 20th livestock census in the country.
- According to estimates of the Central Statistics Office (CSO), the value of the output livestock sector at current prices was about ₹ 5,91691 crore during 2015-16 which is about 28.5% of the value of output from agricultural and allied sectors.
- India accounts for about 17% of the cattle population and 64% of the buffalo population. India is the largest producer of milk in the world.

Fisheries Sector

- India has a coastline of 7516.6 km (6100 km of mainland coastline and coastline of 1197 km Indian islands) touching 13 States and Union Territories (UTs).
- Indian ocean is the least exploited of all the oceans in the world in terms of fishing.
- In India, 75% of marine fish production comes from the West coast.
- As of 2023, India is the third largest fish producing and Second largest aquaculture nation in the world.
- The Indian fisheries sector is a sunrise sector. India is also a major producer of fish through aquaculture and ranks second in the world after China.
- According to Food and Agricultural Organisation (FAO), India is home to more than 10% of the global fish diversity. India has achieved a record fish production of 175.45 lakh tonnes in FY 2022-23. Andhra Pradesh is the largest producer of fish in India followed by West Bengal.

Horticulture

- It is the branch of agriculture concerned with intensively cultured plants directly used by man for food, medicinal purposes and aesthetic gratification.
- In other words, it is cultivation, production and sale of **vegetables, fruits, flowers, herbs**, ornamental or exotic plants.

Floriculture

- It is a branch of horticulture that deals with the cultivation, processing and marketing of ornamental plants vis-a-vis landscaping of small or large areas. It involves maintenance of gardens so that the surroundings may appear aesthetically pleasant.
- The mission will focus on commercial floral crops, seasonal/annual crops, wild ornaments and cultivation of flower crops for honey bee rearing.
- Some of the popular crops includes Gladiolus, Canna, Carnation, Chrysanthemum, Gerbera, Lilium, Marigold, Rose, Tuberose, etc.

Government Steps Related to Agricultural Allied Sectors

- **Horticulture Cluster Development Programme** The Ministry of Agriculture and Farmers Welfare launched the Horticulture Cluster Development Programme (HCDP) on 31st May, 2021 to promote the export of horticultural produce.

  It is a central sector programme aimed at growing and developing identified horticulture clusters to make them globally competitive. It will be implemented by the National Horticulture Board (NHB) of the Ministry of Agriculture and Farmers' Welfare.
- **Kisan Sarathi** Indian Council of Agriculture Research (ICAR) celebrated its 93rd foundation day on 16th July, 2021 and on the occasion, the Kisan Sarathi platform was launched. It was jointly launched by the Union Minister for Agriculture and Farmers' Welfare and the Union Minister of Electronics and Information Technology. It will help farmers to interact and avail personalised advisories on agriculture and allied areas directly from the respective scientists of Krishi Vigyan Kendra (KVKs).
- **Pradhan Mantri Matsya Sampada Yojana** This scheme was launched for Sustainable Development of Fisheries sector on 10th September, 2020 as part of Atma Nirbhar Bharat Package.

  The investment of ₹ 20,000 crores under PMMSY is the highest ever in the fisheries sector. Out of this, an investment of about ₹ 11,000 crores is proposed for beneficiary oriented activities in marine, Inland fisheries and aquaculture and about 9000 crores investment is proposed for fisheries infrastructure.
- **Agriculture Infrastructure Fund** It was launched in 2020 as a part of the stimulus package of ₹ 20 lakh crore announced in response to the Covid-19 crisis.

  It aims to provide medium-long term debt financing facility for investment in viable projects for post-harvest management infrastructure and community farming assets.
- **Biotech-KISAN Programme** It is a scientist-farmer partnership scheme launched in 2017. The Ministry of Science and Technology has issued a special call for the North-East region as a part of its Mission Programme 'Biotech-Krishi Innovation Science Application Network (Biotech-KISAN)'.
- **Aroma Mission and Floriculture Mission** The Union Minister of State Science and Technology has proposed Integrated Aroma Dairy Entrepreneurship for Jammu and Kashmir to augment the income of farmers in the year 2016. The Aroma Mission, also popularly referred as 'Lavender or Purple Revolution', has started from Jammu Kashmir and transformed the lives of farmers who are able to grow lavender, make lucrative profit and improve their lives. Earlier, the floriculture mission was launched in 21 states and Union Territories.
- **National Gene Bank** Gene Banks are a type of bio-repository which preserve genetic material, a collection of seed plants, tissue cultures, etc.
- The Union Minister for Agriculture and Farmers Welfare inaugurated the world's second-largest refurbished state-of-the-art National Gene Bank at the National Bureau of Plant Genetic Resources (NBPGR) in the year 1996.

Agricultural Institutions

Various agricultural institutions are as follows:

Indian Council for Agricultural Research (ICAR)

- The Indian Council for Agricultural Research (ICAR) was established on 16th July, 1929 as a registered society under the Societies Registration Act, 1860.
- It is an autonomous organisation under the Department of Agricultural Research and Education (DARE), Ministry of Agriculture and Farmers Welfare, Government of India.
- It is headquartered at New Delhi with 102 ICAR institutes and 71 agricultural universities spread across the country, this is one of the largest national agricultural systems in the world.
- It is the apex body for coordinating, guiding and managing research and education in agriculture including horticulture, fisheries and animal sciences in the entire country.
- The ICAR has played a pioneering role in promoting Green Revolution and subsequent developments in agriculture in India. Through its research and technology development, it has enabled the country to increase the production of foodgrains, horticultural crops, fish, milk and eggs since 1950-51.

> **Food and Agriculture Organisation (FAO)**
>
> - FAO is a specialised agency of the United Nations that leads international efforts to defeat hunger.
> - World Food Day is celebrated every year on 16th October to mark the anniversary of the FAO in 1945.
> - It is one of the UN Food Aid Organisations based in Rome (Italy). Its sister bodies are the World Food Programme and the International Fund for Agricultural Development (IFAD).

Council for Advancement of People Action and Rural Technology (CAPART)

It is an autonomous body set up by the Ministry of Rural Development to interface between the Government and NGOs that seek to improve the quality of life in rural areas. It was constituted on 1st September, 1986.

National Cooperative Development Corporation (NCDC)

- It is a statutory corporation set up under an Act of Indian Parliament on 13th March, 1963.
- Its objectives are planning and promoting programmes for production, processing, marketing, storage, export, import of agricultural produce, etc.

National Agricultural Cooperative Marketing Federation of India Ltd (NAFED)

- NAFED is an apex organisation of marketing cooperatives for agricultural produce in India. It was established on 2nd October, 1958.
- NAFED is the nodal agency to implement price stabilisation measures under 'Operation Greens' which aims to double the farmers' income by 2022.

Agricultural and Processed Food Products Export Development Authority (APEDA)

- It was established by the Government of India under the Agricultural and Processed Food Products Export Development Authority Act, 1985. It was established on 13th February, 1986.
- It functions under the Ministry of Commerce and Industry. The Authority has its headquarters in New Delhi.
- APEDA is mandated with the responsibility of export, promotion and development of the scheduled products *viz.*
  - Fruits, vegetables and their products;
  - Meat and meat products; poultry and poultry Products; dairy products;
  - Confectionery, biscuits and bakery products;
  - Honey, jaggery and sugar products;
  - Cocoa and its products, chocolates of all kinds; alcoholic and non-alcoholic beverages;
  - Cereal and cereal products;
  - Groundnuts, peanuts and walnuts, pickles, papads and chutneys;
  - Guar gum;
  - Floriculture and floriculture products; herbal and medicinal plants.

Tribal Co-operative Marketing Development Federation of India (TRIFED)

- It came into existence in 1987. It is a national-level apex organisation functioning under the administrative control of the Ministry of Tribal Affairs.
- TRIFED has its Head Office located in New Delhi and has a network of 13 Regional Offices located at various places in the country.
- The ultimate objective of TRIFED is socio-economic development of tribal people in the country by way of marketing development of the tribal products such as metal craft, tribal textiles, pottery, tribal paintings and pottery on which the tribals depend heavily for a major portion of their income.

Agriculture Technology Infrastructure Fund

- For promoting, agricultural distribution at national level, Agriculture Technology Infrastructure Fund was established in the year 2015. Agriculture and Farmers' Welfare Ministry promotes this fund for providing basic agricultural techniques to the farmers.

Agri Export Zones (AEZs)

- Under Export-Import Policy, in the year 2001-02, eight new Agri Export Zones were established in seven states.
- In India, more than 60 Agri Export Zones have been established till now. Among them, some prominent ones are Madhya Pradesh for spices, Uttarakhand for Basmati rice, West Bengal and Tamil Nadu for mango, West Bengal for green vegetables, Maharashtra for onion, etc.

Agriculture in Five Years Plans

- **First Five Year Plan** (1951-1956) Under this plan, the agriculture sector was given priority, 31% of the total revenue allocation was provided to the agriculture sector.
  - Under this plan, the average annual production was 67 lakh tonnes.
  - The agriculture sector registered a growth of 2.71% in this Five Year Plan.
  - During this plan, the major emphasis was given in construction of dams and improving the irrigation facilities for agriculture purposes.
  - Work on projects like Bhakra Nangal dam, Hirakud dam was started in this period.
- **Second Five Year Plan** (1956-1961) A total of 20% revenue was allocated to agriculture sector in this plan. During this time, the productivity remained less, because industries were the focus point.
- **Third Five Year Plan** (1961-1966) In this plan, agriculture was again back in focus, intensive agriculture programme and High Yield Varieties (HYVS) of seeds were promoted in agri-based districts. The effects of Green Revolution started giving positive results, during the period and the production of wheat improved.
- **Fourth Five Year Plan** (1969-1974) In this plan, special emphasis was laid to plan research in agriculture through science and technology, that helped in advancement of agriculture sector. This plan was based on Ashok Rudra and AS Mannis Model.
- **Fifth Five Year Plan** (1974-1979) 15% revenue was allotted for agriculture sector during this plan. 1,520 lakhs tonnes was the target for food production, but the results achieved were more than that.
- **Sixth Five Year Plan** (1980-1985) The second part of **Green Revolution** was started during this plan, with major emphasis on investment in agriculture sector. The entire focus of this plan was on population control and modernisation.
- **Seventh Five Year Plan** (1985-1990) Other than cotton production, all the other crops exceeded the setted targets. Modernisation in agriculture sector was able to reduce the poverty prevailing in rural areas.
- **Eighth Five Year Plan** (1992-1997) During this period, agriculture growth was at 4.7‰ Liberalisation, Privatisation and Globalisation were the major focus of this plan, not much attention was paid in the field of agriculture.
- **Ninth Five Year Plan** (1997-2002) Agriculture sector grew at 2.06% during this period. Rural development along with agriculture and generating employment opportunities were the major points of focus during this period.
- **Tenth Five Year Plan** (2002-2007) National Agriculture Policy, 2000 was adopted during this plan. Special emphasis were given on soil, health and management of water resources.
- **Eleventh Five Year Plan** (2007-2012) A target of 4% annual growth rate was set during this plan. The major objectives of this plan were growth in agriculture productivity, employment generation, population pressure on land, etc.
- **Twelfth Five Year Plan** (2012-2017) 4% annual growth rate was the target set for agriculture sector, in which technology as engine of growth was declared for agriculture sector.

Agricultural Revolutions

Various agricultural revolutions are as follows:

Green Revolution

- Green Revolution was expanded in two phases, first was from 1960s to mid 1970s and the second phase was from the mid 1970s to mid 1980s.
- An American agronomist **Norman Borlaug** started the Green Revolution in the 1960s, he is considered as the 'Father of Green Revolution'. In India, Green Revolution was led by **MS Swaminathan.**
- Due to spread of technology in Green Revolution, India is able to achieve self-reliance in production of food grains. Now, India is no longer dependent on imports of food grains.
- The Green Revolution has increased the income of the farmers and reduced their dependency on the monsoon.
- Green Revolution ended the agricultural stagnation of the colonial period, it was due to the use of High Yielding Varieties of seeds (HYV-seeds).

- The irrigation facilities and use of fertilisers has enhanced the agriculture productivity in India, which helped in rise of wheat and rice production in the country.

White Revolution

- The programme for increasing the production of milk in the country is called as White Revolution. The government launched **'Operation Flood'** to intensify the speed in White Revolution.
- 'Operation Flood' was launched on 13th January, 1970 and **Dr. Verghese Kurien** was the lead person to promote it. He is called the **'Father of White Revolution'** in India.

Blue Revolution

- Progress made in the field of fish production is called as Blue Revolution. India is the third largest country in the world in the field of fish production. The Blue Revolution was initiated through one package programme in the 1960s.
- Its expansion in India is increased during the Seventh Five Year Plan. With the help of World Bank, the one package programme was first implemented in 5 coastal states of India.
- As per 2020-21, the total fish production in the country was 14.16 million tonnes.

Second Green Revolution

- In 2006, A Science conference was to counter the ill effects of first Green Revolution and to ensure the holistic development in the agriculture sector keeping in view the environmental interests. **Dr. APJ Abdul Kalam** started the Second Green Revolution in the country. Under this, the seed selection is done on the basis of land.
- In Second Green Revolution through the medium of Biotechnology and genetic engineering the emphasis was laid upon development of high productivity and quality of seeds.

Evergreen Revolution

- Renowned agricultural scientists **Dr. MS Swaminathan** conceptualised the Evergreen Revolution in year 2006.
- The focus of the Evergreen Revolution is the achievement of the goal of sustainable agriculture development with present perspective the Blue, Green, Yellow, Pink, White and Brown Revolutions are also included under the Evergreen Revolution.
- The main objective of the Evergreen Revolution is to increase productivity, along with relying on products which are environmentally safe, economically viable and socially sustainable.

Important Revolutions of Indian Agriculture and Allied Sector

Revolution	Father of the Revolution	Products/Objectives
Evergreen Revolution	MS Swaminathan	Integration of ecological principles in technology development
Protein Revolution	Coined by Narendra Modi and Arun Jaitley	Higher Production (Technology-driven Second Green Revolution)
Yellow Revolution	Sam Pitroda	Oilseed Production (Especially Mustard and Sunflower)
Black Revolution	–	Petroleum products
Blue Revolution	Dr. Arun Krishnan and Hiralal Chaudhary	Fish Production
Brown Revolution	–	Leather / Cocoa / Non-Conventional Products
Golden Fiber Revolution	–	Jute Production
Golden Revolution	Nirpakh Tutej	Fruits / Honey Production / Horticulture Development
Grey Revolution	M.S. Swaminathan	Fertilisers
Pink Revolution	Durgesh Patel	Onion Production / Pharmaceuticals / Prawn Production
Silver Revolution	Indira Gandhi (Mother of the Revolution)	Egg Production / Poultry Production
Silver Fiber Revolution	–	Cotton
Red Revolution	Vishal Tewari	Meat Production / Tomato Production
Round Revolution	–	Potato
Green Revolution	MS Swaminathan	Food Grains
White Revolution	Verghese Kurien	Milk Production

Extra Facts From Tamil Nadu Board and NIOS

Agricultural Produce Market Committee

- It is a statutory body constituted by state government in order to trade in agricultural or horticultural or livestock products.
- **Functions of APMC** To promote public private partnership in the ambit of agricultural markets.
  - To provide market led extension services to farmer.
  - To bring transparency in pricing system and transactions taking place in market in a transparent manner.
  - To ensure payments to the farmers for the sale of agricultural produce on the same day
  - To promote agricultural activities.
  - To display data on arrivals and rates of agricultural produce from time to timein the market prevailing

Kisan Credit Card Scheme

- A Kisan Credit Card (KCC) is a credit delivery mechanism that is aimed at enabling farmers to have quick and timely access to affordable credit. It was launched in 1998 by the Reserve Bank of India and NABARD.
- It aims to reduce farmer's dependence on the informal banking sector for credit . which can be very expensive and suck them into a debt spiral.
- The card is offered by cooperative banks, regional rural banks and public sector banks. Based on a review of the working of the KCC, the government has advised banks to convert the KCC into a smart card cum debit card.

Green Revolution

- **Achievement of Green Revolution**
  - The major achievement of the new strategy was to boost the production of major cereals viz., wheat and rice.
  - The Green revolution was confined only to High Yielding Varieties (HYV) cereals, mainly rice, wheat, maize and jowar.
  - This Strategy was also directed to increase the production of commercial crops or cash crops such as sugarcane, cotton, jute, oilseeds and potatoes.
  - Per hectare productivity of all crops had increased due to better seeds.
  - Green Revolution had positive effect on development of industries, which manufactured agricultural tools like tractors, engines, threshers and pumping sets.
  - Green Revolution had brought prosperity to rural people. Increased production had generated employment opportunities for rural masses
- **Weaknesses of Green Revolution**
  - Indian Agriculture was still a gamble of the monsoons.
  - This strategy needed heavy investment in seeds, fertilizers, pesticides and water.
  - The income gap between large, marginal and small farmers had increased. Gap between irrigated and rain fed areas had widened.
  - Except in Punjab, and to some extent in Haryana, farm mechanization had created widespread unemployment among agricultural labourers in the rural areas.
  - Larger chemical use and inorganic materials reduced the soil fertility and spoiled human health. Now organic farming is encouraged.

Seed Ball

- A seed ball (or seed bomb) is a seed that has been wrapped in soil materials, usually a mixture of clay and compost, and then dried.
- Essentially, the seed is 'pre-planted' and can be sown by depositing the seed ball anywhere suitable for the species, keeping the seed safely until the proper germination window arises.
- Seed balls are an easy and sustainable way to cultivate plants that provide a larger window of time when the sowing can occur.

Alkali Farming

- Nearly 50 percent of the irrigated land in the arid and semi-arid regions has some
- degree of soil salinization problems. It is found in States of Punjab, Haryana, Uttar Pradesh and Bihar.
- The occurrence of accumulation of excess salt/ acid in the root zone, results in a partial or complete loss of soil productivity and such soil is defined as 'alkali, saline & acid Soils' and exist mainly in arid and semi-arid regions.

07

Industry and Industrial Policies

(SOURCES)

Class-IX & X Old NCERT Chap 4 (Towards Economic Development), Chap 5 (The State and Economic Development), Class-XI New NCERT Chap 1 (Indian Economy on the Eve of Independence, Chap 2 (Indian Economy 1950-1990), Chap 3 (Liberalisation, Privatisation and Globalisation : An Appraisal)

Industry

- Industry refers to an economic activity concerned with the processing of raw materials and manufacture of goods in factories.
- Industries are often classified based on their principal products e.g. steel industry, automobile industry, textile industry, etc.
- The **secondary sector** covers activities in which natural products are changed into other forms through ways of manufacturing that we associate with industrial activity.
- Since, this sector gradually became associated with the different kinds of industries, it is also called the **industrial sector**.

Industrial Development in India

- Industrial development is important for economic development and economic prosperity of a country.
- For enhancing the national income of the country industrialisation plays a major role.
- The Indian Government has been trying to promote rapid industrial growth since independence.
- As a result of various efforts, the industrial sector in India has grown in multifarious dimensions.
- As industry provides employment which is more stable than the employment in agriculture along with modernisation and overall prosperity.
- Due to this, the Five Year Plans emphasised a lot on industrial development.

Industrial Sectors in India

The Industrial sector of the Indian economy is divided into three sectors.

1. Public Sector

- All the enterprises under public sector are government-owned.
- Some of the enterprises under public sector are postal, railway, telegram, etc. These enterprises are under different ministries.
- In addition, there are also non-departmental enterprises whose establishment are in the form of public issues under act passed by Parliament.
- The purpose of public sector is not only to make profit, but also public welfare activities.

2. Private Sector

- Enterprises coming under the private sector has a private ownership.
- After independence, India adopted the mixed economy policy under which private sector plays an important role.
- In the Industrial Policy of 1956, private sector is placed under major industries.
- The private sector in India is very wide, countries most important economic activity i.e. agriculture is completely under private sector.

- **Tata Iron and Steel Company Limited** (TISCO) and Reliance companies are India's major privately owned enterprises.

3. Joint Sector

- Joint sector is a type of partnership between private and public sector. The control, management and ownership of joint sector enterprises distributed between the government and private.
- In 1969, under the leadership of **Subimal Dutt** the 'Industrial licensing Policy Inquiring Committee' or 'Dutt Committee' was established, to follow up reports of Monopolies Inquiry Commission and Hazari Committee.

Industrial Policy

- For the balanced industrial growth, industrial policy is essential. **Department for Promotion of Industry and Internal Trade** (DPIIT) is responsible for the formulation of industrial policies.
- Government actions influence the ownership and structure of the industry and its performance in the form of paying subsidies, providing finance, imposing regulation, etc.
- It includes procedures, principles (i.e., the philosophy of a given economy), policies, rules and regulations, incentives and punishments, the tariff policy, the labour policy, government's attitude towards foreign capital, etc.
- The **main objectives** of the Industrial Policy of the Government in India are:
  - To maintain a sustained growth in productivity,
  - To enhance gainful employment,
  - To achieve optimal utilisation of human resources,
  - To attain international competitiveness,
  - To transform India into a major partner and player in the global arena.

Industrial Policies in India Since Independence

Since Independence, many industrial policies have been implemented. These are discussed as follows :

Industrial Policy Resolution, 1948

- First industrial policy was announced in April 1948 by then Industrial Minister late **Shyama Prasad Mukherjee.**
- It defined the broad contours of the policy delineating the role of the nation in industrial development both as an entrepreneur and authority. It made clear that India is going to have a **Mixed Economic Model**.
- The Industries (Development and Regulation) Act was passed in 1951 to implement the **Industrial Policy Resolution** (IPR), 1948.
- It classified industries into **four broad areas** :

(i) **Strategic Industries** (Public Sector) It included three industries in which Central Government had a monopoly. These included Arms and ammunition, Atomic energy and Rail transport.

(ii) **Basic/Key Industries** (Public-cum-Private Sector) Six industries *viz.* coal, iron and steel, aircraft manufacturing, ship-building, manufacture of telephone, telegraph and wireless apparatus and mineral oil were designated as 'Key Industries' or 'Basic Industries'.

These industries were to be set-up by the Central Government. However, the existing private sector enterprises were allowed to continue.

(iii) **Important Industries** (Controlled Private Sector)

It included 18 industries including heavy chemicals, sugar, cotton textile and woollen industry, cement, paper, salt, machine tools, fertiliser, rubber, air and sea transport, motor, tractor, electricity, etc.

These industries continue to remain under the private sector. However, the Central Government, in consultation with the State Government, had general control over them.

(iv) **Other Industries** (Private and Cooperative Sector)

All other industries which were not included in the above-mentioned three categories were left open for the private sector.

Industrial Policy Resolution, 1956

- Government revised its first Industrial Policy (i.e. the policy of 1948) through the Industrial Policy of 1956.
- It was regarded as the 'Economic Constitution of India' or **The Bible of State Capitalism.**
- The 1956 Policy emphasised the need to expand the public sector, to build up a large and growing cooperative sector and to encourage the separation of ownership and management in private industries and, above all, prevent the rise of private monopolies.
- It provided the basic framework for the government's policy in regard to industries till June 1991.
- The Industrial Policy Resolution 1956, stressed the importance of cottage and small scale industries for expanding employment opportunities and for wider decentralisation of economic power and activity.
- Industrial Policy Resolution, 1956 classified industries into three categories :
  - **Schedule A** consisting of 17 industries was the exclusive responsibility of the state. Out of these 17 industries, four industries, namely arms and

ammunition, atomic energy, railways and air transport had Central Government monopolies; new units in the remaining industries were developed by the State Governments.

- **Schedule B** Consisting of 12 industries, was open to both the private and public sectors; however, such industries were progressively state-owned.
- **Schedule C** All the other industries not included in the above two schedules constituted the third category which was left open to the private sector. However, the State reserved the right to undertake any type of industrial production.

Industrial Licencing

- In order to open new industry or to expand production, obtaining a license from the government was a prerequisite.
- Opening new industries in economically backward areas was incentivised through easy licensing and subsidisation of critical inputs like electricity and water. This was done to counter regional disparities that existed in the country.
- Licences to increase production were issued only if the government was convinced that the economy required more of the goods.

Industrial Policy, 1977

Industrial Policy, 1977 was announced in December, 1977 through a statement in the Parliament. Some of the important **provisions** of the policy are as follows :

- The main thrust of this policy was the effective promotion of cottage and small industries widely dispersed in rural areas and small towns.
- In this policy, the small sector was classified into three groups i.e., cottage and household sector, tiny sector and small scale industries.
- It prescribed different areas for the large scale industrial sector i.e., Basic industries, Capital goods industries, High technology industries and other industries outside the list of reserved items for the small scale sector.
- It restricted the scope of large business houses so that no unit of the same business group acquired a dominant and monopolistic position in the market.
- It put emphasis on reducing the occurrence of labour unrest. The Government encouraged the worker's participation in management from shop floor level to board level.

Industrial Policy, 1980

- This policy was adopted on 23rd July, 1980. Its main objective was to facilitate an increase in industrial production through optimum utilisation of installed capacity and expansion of industries.
- It aimed to reverse the trend of industrial production of the past three years and reaffirmed its faith in the **Monopolies and Restrictive Trade Practices** (MRTP) Act and the **Foreign Exchange Regulation** Act, (FERA).

New Industrial Policy, 1991

- The long-awaited liberalised industrial policy was announced by the Government of India in 1991, in the midst of severe economic instability in the country.
- The objective of the policy was to raise efficiency and accelerate economic growth.

Features of New Industrial Policy

Various features of New Industrial Policy are as follows :

1. De-reservation of Public Sector

- Sectors that were earlier exclusively reserved for the public sector were reduced.
- However, the pre-eminent place of public sector in 5 core areas like arms and ammunition, atomic energy, mineral oils, rail transport and mining was continued.
- Presently, only two sectors Atomic Energy and Railway Operations are reserved exclusively for the public sector.

2. De-licensing

- Abolition of Industrial licensing for all projects except for a short list of industries.
- There are only six industries at present related to security, strategic and environmental concerns, where an industrial licence is required.

  These are :
  (i) Distillation and brewing of alcoholic drinks
  (ii) Cigars and Cigarettes
  (iii) Electronic aerospace and defence equipment
  (iv) Industrial explosives
  (v) Hazardous chemicals
  (vi) Drugs and pharmaceuticals

3. Disinvestment of Public Sector

Government stakes in Public Sector Enterprises were reduced to enhance their efficiency and competitiveness.

4. Liberalisation of Foreign Investment

- This was the first Industrial policy in which foreign companies were allowed to have majority stake in India. In 47 high priority industries, upto 51% FDI was allowed.
- For export trading houses, FDI upto 74% was allowed. Today, there are numerous sectors in the economy where the government allows 100% FDI.
- **Foreign Technology Agreement** automatically gives approvals for technology related agreements.

5. Fair Trade

- The Monopolistic and Restrictive Trade Practices Act, was amended to remove the threshold limits of assets in respect of MRTP companies and dominant undertakings. The MRTP Act was replaced by the Competition Act, 2002.

Outcomes of New Industrial Policy

- The 1991 policy made 'Licence, Permit and Quota Raj' a thing of the past.
- It attempted to liberalise the economy by removing bureaucratic hurdles in industrial growth.
- Limited role of the Public sector reduced the burden of the Government.
- Easy entry of Multinational Companies, privatisation, removal of assets limits on MRTP companies, liberal licensing etc were some of the key features of the policy.
- All this resulted in increased competition that led to lower prices in many goods such as electronics prices. This brought domestic as well as foreign investment in almost every sector opened to the private sector.
- The policy was followed by special efforts to increase exports.
- Concepts like Export Oriented Units, Export Processing Zones, Agri-Export Zones, Special Economic Zones and lately National Investment and Manufacturing Zones emerged. All these have benefitted the export sector of the country.

National Manufacturing Policy (NMP), 2011

The major objectives of the National Manufacturing Policy (NMP), 2011 are as follows :

- To increase the sectoral share of manufacturing in GDP to atleast 25% by the year 2022.
- To increase the rate of job creation so as to create 100 million additional jobs by the year 2022.
- To enhance global competitiveness, domestic value addition, technological depth and environmental sustainability of growth.
- To provide a productive environment to persons transitioning from the primary to the secondary and tertiary sectors by creating **National Investment and Manufacturing Zones** (NIMZs).
- To ensure compliance of labour and environmental laws while introducing procedural simplifications and rationalisation, so that the regulatory burden on industry is reduced.
- To provide an enabling environment for tapping the potential of the private sector and the entrepreneurial skills of the younger population.

Companies Act, 2013

- This act introduced significant changes in the provisions related to governance, e-management, compliance and enforcement, disclosure norms, auditors and mergers and acquisitions. New concepts such as one-person company, small companies, dormant company, class action suits, registered valuers and **Corporate Social Responsibility** (CSR) have also been included.
- The 2013 Act has introduced several new concepts and has also tried to streamline many of the requirements by introducing new definitions i.e., :
  - **One-Person Company** The 2013 Act introduces a new type of entity to the existing list i.e. apart from forming a public or private limited company, the 2013 Act enables the formation of a new entity, a 'One-Person Company' (OPC).
  - **Small Company** A small company has been defined as a company, other than a public company. Paid-up share capital of which does not exceed ₹ 50 lakh. Turnover of which as per its last profit and loss account does not exceed ₹ 2 crore or such higher amount as may be prescribed which shall not be more than ₹ 20 crore.
  - **Dormant Company** The 2013 Act states that a company can be classified as dormant when it is formed and registered under this 2013 Act for a future project or to hold an asset or intellectual property and has no significant accounting transaction.
  - **National Financial Reporting Authority** (NFRA) The 2013 Act requires the Constitution of NFRA, which has been bestowed with significant powers not only in issuing the authoritative pronouncements, but also in regulating the audit profession.
  - **Serious Fraud Investigation Office** (SFIO) The 2013 Act has bestowed legal status to SFIO.
  - **Corporate Social Responsibility** The 2013 Act makes an effort to introduce the culture of Corporate Social Responsibility (CSR) in Indian corporates by requiring companies to formulate a corporate social responsibility policy and atleast incur a given minimum expenditure on social activities.

Companies Amendment Act, 2020

- This bill was introduced in the Parliament in March 2020 to further the government's agenda of Ease of Doing Business (EoDB) and also to decriminalise the Companies Law Act, 2013.
- President of India gave his assent to the bill on 28th September, 2020.

- Some key amendments, as proposed by this Act are given below :
- In context of offences it makes three changes, i.e.,
  (i) penalties for few offences have been removed,
  (ii) imprisonment for few offences has been removed
  (iii) the amount of fine payable in certain offences has been also reduced.
  - It empowers the government to allow certain classes of public companies to list classes of securities (as may be prescribed) in foreign jurisdictions.
  - Earlier a person holding at least 10% of company's share was required to make a declaration of his interest to the company.
  - To reduce compliances and boost EoDB, this amendment empowers government to exempt any class of persons from complying with these requirements.
  - It empowers the government to require classes of unlisted companies to prepare and file periodical financial results, and to complete the audit or review of such results. The provision related with remuneration of executive director even in the year when company has not registered any profit has been extended to non-executive directors, including independent directors.

Contribution of Different Industries in Economy

- According to the 2021 Report of World Steel Association, India ranks second in the production of steel after China. Japan stands third in the world production of steel.
- Steel industry provides employment to around 25 lakh people in India, which is 2% of the India's Gross Domestic Product (GDP).
- Automobile industry contributes 7.1% to India's GDP. This share of automobile industry is 49% in India's manufacturing industries sector for its special contribution in the Indian Economy, automobile industry is also known as **Sunrise Industry**.
- Textile industry contributes 4% to the India's GDP and 11% to foreign income. Chemical industry contributes 3% to the India's GDP and Indian Chemical Industry is ranked sixth in the world.

Measures of Industrial Production

Industrial production in India is measured broadly by the following indicators :

Purchasing Managers' Index (PMI)

- Purchasing Managers' Index (PMI) is an indicator of business activity-both in the manufacturing and services sectors.
- It is calculated separately for the manufacturing and services sectors and then a composite index is also constructed.
- The PMI summarises whether market conditions as viewed by purchasing managers are expanding, neutral or contracting.
- The purpose of the PMI is to provide information about current and future business conditions to company decision makers, analysts and investors.
- The PMI is a number from 0 to 100.
- PMI above 50 represents an expansion when compared to the previous month; PMI under 50 represents a contraction and a reading at 50 indicates no change.
- The PMI is usually released at the start of every month. It is, therefore, considered a good leading indicator of economic activity.
- It is different from the Index of Industrial Production (IIP), which also gauges the level of activity in the economy.

Index of Industrial Production (IIP)

- It is an index which helps us understand the growth of various sectors in the Indian economy such as mining, electricity and manufacturing.
- IIP is a short-term indicator of industrial growth till the results from Annual Survey of Industries (ASI) and National Accounts Statistics (e.g. GDP) are available.
- The base year of the index is given a value of 100.
- The current base year for the IIP series in India is 2011-12. When the current IIP reads 180, it means that there has been 80% industrial growth compared to the base year, i.e. 2011-12.
- Index of Industrial Production (IIP) is released by the National Statistics Office (NSO) of the Ministry of Statistics and Programme Implementation.
- IIP is published monthly and six weeks after the reference month ends.

Difference Between PMI and IIP

- IIP covers the broader industrial sector compared to PMI.
- IIP shows the change in production volume in major industrial sub sectors like manufacturing, mining and electricity.
- Similarly, the IIP also gives use based (capital goods, consumer goods, etc) trends in industrial production.
- PMI is more dynamic compared to a standard industrial production index.
- The PMI can sense dynamic trends as it uses variables for the construction of the index as compared to volume based production indicators of IIP.

Annual Survey of Industries (ASI)

- ASI is calculated on an annual basis. The ASI has been conducted under the **Collection of Statistics Act**, since 1959.
- The objective is to obtain comprehensive and detailed statistics of industrial sector with the objective of estimating the contribution of registered manufacturing industries as a whole to the national income.
- ASI data is based on the actual book of accounts and other documents maintained by registered factories.

Public Sector Undertakings

- In our country, a Public Sector Undertaking (PSU) is a government-owned corporation. These companies are owned and operated by the Union Government of India or a State Government individually or collectively.
- The equity of such company is majorly owned by the government, hence named PSU.
- The need for setting up of PSUs arises because industrial development of any country requires a strong foundation supported by reliable infrastructure.
- After economic reforms, various PSUs have been awarded additional financial autonomy by the Government.
- The PSUs are divided into the following three categories :
  (a) Maharatna
  (b) Navratna
  (c) Miniratna Category - I and II

Criteria for Grant of Maharatna Status

- This category was granted in 2009. Maharatna status shall be given to Central Public Sector Enterprises (CPSEs) :
  - Having Navratna status.
  - Listed on Indian stock exchange with minimum prescribed public shareholding under SEBI regulations.
  - Average annual turnover of more than ₹ 25,000 crore, during the last 3 years.
  - Average annual net worth of more than ₹ 15,000 crore, during the last 3 years.
  - Average annual net profit after tax of more than ₹ 5,000 crore, during the last 3 years.
  - Should have significant global presence/ international operations.
- Presently there are **13 Maharatna Companies**. The Maharatna CPSEs are as follows :
  1. Oil and Natural Gas Corporation (ONGC) Limited
  2. Indian Oil Corporation Limited (IOCL)
  3. Steel Authority of India Limited (SAIL)
  4. National Thermal Power Corporation (NTPC)
  5. Coal India Limited (CIL)
  6. Bharat Heavy Electrical Limited (BHEL)
  7. Gas Authority of India Limited (GAIL)
  8. Bharat Petroleum Corporation Limited (BPCL)
  9. Hindustan Petroleum Corporation Limited (HPCL)
  10. Power Grid Corporation of India Limited (PGCIL)
  11. Power Finance Corporation Limited (PFCL)
  12. Rural Electrification Corporation Limited (RECL)
  13. Oil India Limited (OIL)

Criteria for Grant of Navratna Status

- This category was started in 1997. The Miniratna Category – I and Schedule 'A' CPSEs, which have obtained 'excellent' or 'very good' rating under the Memorandum of Understanding system in three of the last five years and have composite score of 60 or above in the six selected performance parameters, namely :
  - net profit to net worth.
  - manpower cost to total cost of production/services.
  - profit before depreciation, interest and taxes to capital employed.
  - profit before interest and taxes to turnover.
  - earning per share.
  - inter-sectoral performance.
- Presently there are **16 Navratna Companies**. Navratna CPSEs are as follows :
  - Bharat Electronics Limited (BEL)
  - Hindustan Aeronautics Limited (HAL)
  - Mahanagar Telephone Nigam Limited (MTNL)
  - National Aluminium Company Limited (NACL)
  - National Mineral Development Corporation (NMDC) Limited
  - Rashtriya Ispat Nigam Limited (RINL)
  - Shipping Corporation of India Limited (SCIL)
  - Neyveli Lignite Corporation Limited (NLCL)
  - Container Corporation of India Limited (CONCOR)
  - Engineers India Limited (EIL)
  - National Buildings Consumption Corporation Limited (NBCCL)
  - Rail India Technical and Economic Services (RITES)
  - Ircon International Limited (IRCON)
  - Rail Vikash Nigam Limited (RVNL)
  - Rashtriya Chemicals and Fertilisers Limited (RCFL)
  - Oil and Natual Gas Corporation Videsh Limited (OVL)

Criteria for Grant of Miniratna Status

- This category was started in 1997. Those CPSEs that have shown profits in the last continuous three years and have positive net worth, can be considered eligible for grant of Miniratna status. Presently, there are total 68 Miniratnas.
- The Miniratnas are divided in two categories–I and II.
  - **Category I** These have made profits for the last three years continuously or earned a net profit of ₹ 30 crores or more in one of these three years. There are 57 companies.
  - **Category II** These companies have made profits continuously for the last three years and must have a positive net worth. There are 11 such companies in this category.

Disinvestment vs Privatisation

Disinvestment refers to selling of equity of a PSU to a private organisation or to general public. Privatisation refers to providing for larger role for private capital and enterprise in the functioning of an economy.

Privatisation is a wider term than disinvestment. Disinvestment is one of the means for achieving privatisation. Privatisation may result from any of the following :

- Disinvestment
- Denationalisation (i.e. complete sell off of a PSUs)
- Transfer of management and control of a PSUs to the private sector
- Dereservation of areas reserved for the public sector, etc.

Large Scale Industries

Large scale industries are referred to as those industries that are having huge infrastructure, raw material, high manpower requirements and large capital requirements. The large-scale industries of India fall broadly into four important classes :

(i) The **basic industries** are those that provide essential inputs to all important industries and agriculture. They comprise coal, iron ore, fertilisers, caustic soda, etc.

(ii) The **Capital goods industries** are those that produce the machinery and equipment for all industries and agriculture. These includes machine tools, industrial machinery, process plant equipment, construction and mining equipment, electrical equipment, textile machinery, printing and packaging machinery, etc.

(iii) The **Intermediate goods industries** produce goods that are used in the process of production in other industries or as accessory to the capital goods in the industries like automobile tyres and petroleum refinery products.

(iv) The **Consumer goods industries** includes textiles, sugar, paper, etc.

Micro, Small and Medium Enterprises (MSME)

- MSMEs have been accepted as the engine of economic growth and for promoting equitable development throughout the world.
- They constitute over 90% of total enterprises in most of the economies and are credited with generating the highest rates of employment growth.
- With low investment requirements, operational flexibility and the capacity to develop appropriate indigenous technology, MSMEs have the power to propel India to new heights. Hence, it seems like there is a silent revolution happening in India powered by MSMEs.
- The Micro, Small and Medium Enterprises Development (Amendment) Bill, 2018 proposes to reclassify all MSMEs, whether they are manufacturing or service-providing enterprises, on the basis of their annual turnover.

Importance of MSMEs for Indian Economy

The following points highlight importance of MSMEs for Indian economy:

- **Employment** It is the second largest employment generating sector after agriculture. It provides employment to around 120 million persons in India.
- **Contribution to GDP** With around 36.1 million units throughout the geographical expanse of the country, MSMEs contribute around 6.11% of the manufacturing GDP and 24.63% of the GDP from service activities.

  MSME ministry has set a target to up its contribution to GDP to 50% by 2025 as to support India's goal of achieving a US $ 5 trillion economy.
- **Exports** It contributes around 45% of the overall exports from India.
- **Inclusive Growth** MSMEs promote inclusive growth by providing employment opportunities in rural areas especially to people belonging to weaker sections of the society. For example, Khadi and Village industries require low per capita investment and employ a large number of women in rural areas.
- **Financial Inclusion** Small industries and retail businesses in tier-II and tier-III cities create opportunities for people to use banking services and products.
- **Promote Innovation** It provides opportunity for budding entrepreneurs to build creative products boosting business competition and fuels growth.

Classification of Enterprises as MSMEs (2020)

Type of Enterprise	Investment in Plant and Machinery or Equipment	Annual Turnover
Micro	₹ 1 crore	₹ 5 crore
Small	₹ 10 crore	₹ 50 crore
Medium	₹ 50 crore	₹ 250 crore

Organisations Related to MSMEs

Some important organisations related to micro, small and medium enterprises are as follows :

Small Industries Development Organisation (SIDO)

- It was founded in the year 1954. SIDO is an apex body and nodal agency for formulating, coordinating and monitoring the policies and programmes for promotion and development of small scale industries.
- It provides services for micro, small and medium industries also.

National Small Industries Corporation Limited

- It is a PSU established by the Government of India in 1955. It falls under Ministry of Micro, Small and Medium Enterprises of India.
- Government of India in order to promote small and budding entrepreneurs of post independent India, decided to establish a government agency which can mediate and provide help to Small Scale Industries (SSI).
- Government had established National Small Industries Corporation with an objective to provide machinery on hire-purchase basis assisting and marketing in exports.

Micro, Small and Medium Enterprises Development Organisation

- It was constituted in 1954 as a Small Industries Development Organisation.
- It works as an apex body for micro, small and medium enterprises.
- It plays a key role in the implementation of programmes and policies of micro, small and medium enterprises.

Schemes Related to MSMEs

Some important schemes related to MSMEs are :

- **Raising and Accelerating MSME Performance (RAMP) Scheme** It is a world Bank assisted Central Sector Scheme aimed at improving access to market and credit.
- It will address the issue of delayed payments and greening of MSMEs.
- **Scheme of Fund for Regeneration of Traditional Industries (SFRUTI)** The Ministry of MSMEs launched this scheme in the year 2005 with the view to promote Cluster development.
- **SFURTI** Its clusters are of two types i.e., Regular Cluster (500 artisans) with Government assistance of up to₹ 2.5 crore and Major Cluster (more than 500 artisans) with Government assistance up to ₹ 5 crore.
- **Udyog Aadhaar Memorandum** (UAM) It is a simple one-page registration form to promote Ease of Doing Business for MSMEs in India.
- **A Scheme for Promoting Innovation, Rural Industry and Entrepreneurship** (ASPIRE) The scheme promotes innovation and rural entrepreneurship through rural Livelihood Business Incubator (LBI), Technology Business Incubator (TBI) and Fund of Funds for start-up creation in the agro-based industry.
- **Credit Guarantee Fund Scheme** To facilitate easy flow of credit, guarantee cover is provided for collateral free credit extended to MSMEs.
- **Prime Minister's Employment Generation Programme** (PMEGP) It is a credit linked subsidy scheme, for setting up of new micro-enterprises and to generate employment opportunities in rural as well as urban areas of the country.
- **Credit Linked Capital Subsidy Scheme** (CLCSS) **for Technology Upgradation** It aims at facilitating technology upgradation of Micro and Small Enterprises (MSMEs) by providing 15% capital subsidy for purchase of plant and machinery.
- **Policy Reforms for Startups** These include requirement of distributable profits for three years for a company to be eligible to issue shares with differential voting rights.
- **Start up Cells** These cells will work towards redressal of grievances and tax-related issues of Startups with respect to the administration of the Income-tax Act, 1961.
- **National Startup Advisory Council** To advise the Centre on measures needed to build a strong ecosystem for nurturing innovation and start-ups in the country.
- **Aatmanirbhar Bharat ARISE-Atal New India Challenge** It is a national initiative to promote research and innovation and increase competitiveness of Indian startups and Micro, Small and Medium Enterprises (MSMEs).
- **AIM-iCREST** It is an Incubator Capabilities Enhancement programme launched by NITI Aayog for a Robust Ecosystem focused on creating high performing Startups.

Abid Hussain Committee on Small Scale Industries

It was appointed to suggest measures for improving the Small-Scale Industries (SSIs). The committee submitted its report in January, 1997.

The main recommendations were as follows :

- The concept of SSI should be widened to include small-scale business and service enterprises.
- Instead of protecting the SSI on the ground of infant industry, they should rather be promoted.
- This policy of promotion should consist of adequate supply of credit, service, technology assistance, infrastructure, low transaction cost, etc.
- Setting up support systems for small enterprises by developing clusters of small enterprises to reap the benefits of informational economies and economies in infrastructure development.
- Abolishing all reserved products which had been earmarked exclusively for SSI.

Central Government Schemes Related to Industrialisation

Important Central Government schemes related to industrialisation are as follows :

National Technical Textile Mission

- The decision to start this mission was taken by Cabinet Committee on Economic Affairs (CCEA) in February, 2020. It aims at taking the domestic market size from $ 40 billion to $ 50 billion by 2024.

FAME India Scheme

- Faster Adoption and Manufacturing of Hybrid and Electric Vehicles (FAME) India Scheme is mainly associated with electric vehicles.
- It was started in the year 2019 and its second edition was launched in June 2021.

Make in India

- The Make in India campaign was launched by the Prime Minister of India on 25th September, 2014.
- Its objectives are as follows :
  - To attract foreign investment for new industrialisation and develop the already existing industry base in India to surpass that of China.
  - Target of an increase in manufacturing sector growth to 12-14% per annum over the medium term.
  - To increase the share of the manufacturing sector in the country's Gross Domestic Product from 16% to 25% by 2022.
  - To create 100 million additional jobs by 2022.
  - To promote export-led growth.

Startup India

- It envisages building a robust Startup ecosystem in the country for nurturing innovation and providing opportunities to budding entrepreneurs.
- It was launched in 2016.
- The action plan of this initiative focuses on following three areas :
  - Simplification and Handholding.
  - Funding Support and Incentives.
  - Industry-Academia Partnership and Incubation.

Stand-up India

- Stand-up India was launched by the Government of India on 5th April, 2016 to support entrepreneurship among women and SC and ST communities.
- The scheme offers bank loans of between ₹ 10 lakh (US$13,000) and ₹ 1 crore (US$130,000) for Scheduled Castes and Scheduled Tribes and women setting up new enterprises outside of the farm sector.

Pradhan Mantri Mudra Yojana (PMMY)

- It was launched by the government in 2015 for providing loans upto ₹ 10 lakh to the non-corporate, non-farm small/micro-enterprises.
- It provides funding to the non-corporate small business sector through various last-mile financial institutions like Banks, Non-Banking Financial Companies (NBFCs) and Micro Finance Institutions (MFIs).
- It has created three products i.e. 'Shishu', 'Kishore' and 'Tarun' as per the stage of growth and funding needs of the beneficiary micro unit.
  - **Shishu** Covering loans upto ₹ 50,000.
  - **Kishore** Covering loans above ₹ 50,000 and upto ₹ 5 lakh.
  - **Tarun** Covering loans above ₹ 5 lakh and upto ₹ 10 lakh.

Eight Core Industries and their Performance

- The Base Year of the Index of Eight Core Industries has been revised from the year 2004-05 to 2011-12 from April, 2017.
- The shift is in line with the new base year of Index of Industrial Production (IIP).
- The industries covered in the Index of Eight Core are namely as Coal, Crude Oil, Natural Gas, Refinery Products, Fertilisers, Steel, Cement and Electricity.

- These remain the same as in the 2004-05 series. The revised Eight Core Industries have a combined weight of 40.27% in the IIP.
- The combined index of Eight Core Industries (ECI) increased by 3.6% (Provisional) in January, 2024 as compared to the Index of January 2023.

The weightage of core industries are as follows :

Industry	Weight age
Electricity	19.85%
Steel (Alloy Non-alloy)	17.92%
Refinery Products	28.04%
Crude Oil	8.98 %
Coal	10.33%
Cement	5.37%
Natural Gas	6.88%
Fertilisers	2.63%

Organisations Related to Industrial Sector

Different organisations related to industrial sector are as follows :

Department for Promotion of Industry and Internal Trade (DPIIT)

- It was established in the year 1995 and was reconstituted in the year 2000 with the merger of the Department of Industrial Development.
- Earlier, separate ministries of Small Scale Industries and Agro and Rural Industries (SSI and ARI) and Heavy Industries and Public Enterprises (HI and PE) were created in October, 1999.
- The department was earlier called Department of Industrial Policy and Promotion and was renamed as DPIIT in January, 2019.
- In 2018, matters related to e-commerce were transferred to the Department and in 2019, the Department has been given charge for matters related to internal trade, welfare of traders and their employees and startups.
- The role of DPIIT is to promote/accelerate industrial development of the country by facilitating investment in new and upcoming technology, foreign direct investment and supporting balanced development of industries.

Small Industries Development Bank of India (SIDBI)

- SIDBI is the principal financial institution for promotion, financing and development of Micro, Small and Medium Enterprises (MSME) sector in India.
- It was established on 2nd April, 1990 through an Act of Parliament (thus, it is a statutory body). It is headquartered in Lucknow, Uttar Pradesh.
- SIDBI aims to facilitate and strengthen credit flow to MSMEs and address both financial and developmental gaps in the MSME ecosystem across the country.
- It co-ordinates functions of institutions engaged in similar activities.
- Currently, the shares of SIDBI are held by the Central Government and 29 other institutions including Public Sector Banks (PSBs), insurance companies owned and controlled by the Central Government.

National Investment Fund (NIF)

- In pursuance of the policy laid down in National Common Minimum Programme (NCMP), the Central Government set-up a National Investment Fund (NIF) in November 2005.
- The proceeds from disinvestment of Central Public Sector Undertakings (CPSUs) will be channelised into NIF, which is to be maintained outside the Consolidated Fund of India.
- NIF will be professionally managed to provide sustainable returns to the government, without depleting the corpus.
- In order to align the NIF with the disinvestment policy, government decided in 2013 that the disinvestment proceeds, with effect from the fiscal year 2013-14, will be credited to the existing NIF which is a public account under the government accounts and the funds would remain there until withdrawn/invested for the approved purposes.

Ease of Doing Business Report

- The report was introduced in 2003 by the World Bank to provide an assessment of objective measures of business regulations and their enforcement across 190 economies on ten parameters affecting a business through its life cycle.
- The report measures the performance of countries across 10 different parameters namely as

(i) Starting a business,
(ii) Dealing with construction permits,
(iii) Electricity availability,
(iv) Property registration,
(v) Credit availability,
(vi) Protecting minority investors,
(vii) Paying taxes,
(viii) Trading across borders,
(ix) Contracts enforcement, and
(x) Resolving insolvency.

- It ranks countries on the basis of Distance To Frontier (DTF) score that highlights the gap of an economy with respect to the global best practice. For example, a score of 75 means an economy was 25% points away from the frontier constructed from the best performances across all economies and across time.

Ease of Doing Business Rankings of the States

- It is released by the Department for Promotion of Industry and Internal Trade (Ministry of Commerce and Industry).
- The rankings were started with an objective of fostering competitiveness, mutual learning and propel states and Union Territories (UTs) to work proactively towards uplifting the startup ecosystem.

Five Year Plans and Industrial Development

Following is a brief description of Five Year Plans and industrial development :

- **First Five Year Plan** (1951-1956) The role of both public and private sectors was acknowledged under this plan. It also started the process of mixed economy. Out of total expenditure 2.8% was provided for industries and mineral sectors.
- **Second Five Year Plan** (1956-1961) Industrialisation was the central focus of the plan. Under this rapid industrial development was ensured with establishment of basic industries. A total of 20.1% of total expenditure was provided to industrial sectors in the Five Year Plan.
- **Third Five Year Plan** (1961-1966) Under this plan, cement and fertilisers industries were established. In this plan, the goals of Second Five Year Plans were pursued. A total of 20.1% of total expenditure was provided during this plan.
- **Fourth Five Year Plan** (1969-1974) Under this plan, development of industries were encouraged more. Under the impact of Green revolution the dynamism in field of agriculture promoted industrialisation. In this Five Year Plan, the expenditure on the industrial sector was 18.2%.
- **Fifth Five Year Plan** (1974-1978) Under this plan, the Minimum Need Programme (MNP) was started. Under this programme in 1975 the Twenty Point Programme (TPP) was also started.
- Under this plan 22.8% of expenditure was incurred of total planned expenditure, which was the highest in comparison to other plans.
- **Sixth Five Year Plan** (1980-1985) Under this plan, the process of liberalisation was started 13.8% was the total expenditure incurred in industrialisation under this plan.
- **Seventh Five Year Plan** (1985-1990) Technological development had positive impact on industries and along with social justice the process of development got speed up.
- In this Five Year Plan, 11.9% of the total revenue was spent on the industrial sector.
- **Eighth Five Year Plan** (1992-1997) The new economic policy, 1999 was implemented in this Five Year Plan.
- Under this plan, 9.3% of the total plan expenditure was provided to the industrial sector.
- **Ninth Five Year Plan** (1997-2002) Importance was given to the industrial sector.
- Under this plan, many new schemes were introduced for enhancement of economic efficiency and capacity. A total 5% expenditure was incurred to industrial sector.
- **Tenth Five Year Plan** (2002-2007) In place of industrial sector investment in the social sector was given importance.
- Only 3.9% of total revenue expenditure was provided for industrial sector, which was the least in comparison of any Five Years Plan.
- **Eleventh Five Year Plan** (2007-2012) Under this five year plan, 10% was set as growth goal for industrial sector 4.5% of total expenditure was given to the industrial sector.
- **Twelfth Five Year Plan** (2012-2017) A target of 9.6% was kept for development of Industries in this Five Year Plan.
- For development in industries, emphasis was given to the infrastructure development.

Extra Facts From Tamil Nadu Board and NIOS

- Rural industries are based to promote agricultural activities mainly on the utilisation of locally available raw materials, skills and small amount of capital. The rural industries can be broadly classified into (a) cottage industries, (b) village industries, (c) small industries, (d) tiny industries and (e) agro-based industries.
- Small Scale Industries are also known as Micro, Small & Medium Enterprises (MSMEs).
- They are defined and categorised by the Micro, Small and Medium Enterprises Development Act, 2006.

Industrial Deregulation

Before	After
Industrial Licensing for all commodities	Licensing restricted to alcohol, drugs, etc
Private sector not allowed in many industries	Only defence, energy, railway for public sector-large scale privatisation, disinvestment
Controls on price fixation and distribution	Market allowed to determine prices

Special Economic Zones (SEZs) Policy was announced in April 2000.

- It was launched to overcome the shortcomings experienced on account of the multiplicity of controls and clearances, absence of world-class infrastructure, and an unstable fiscal regime and with a view to attract larger foreign investments in India.
- India was one of the first in Asia to recognise the effectiveness of the Export Processing Zone (EPZ) model in promoting exports, with Asia's first EPZ set up in Kandla in 1965.
- Main characteristics of SEZ are
  - (a) Geographically demarked area with physical security.
  - (b) Administrated by single body/ authority
  - (c) Streamlined procedures
  - (d) Having separate custom area and
  - (e) Governed by more liberal economic laws.

Iron and Steel Industries First steel industry at Kulti, Near Jharia, West Bengal - Bengal iron works company in 1870. First large scale steal plant TISCO at Jamshedpur in 1907 followed by TISCO at Burnpur in 1919. Both belonged to private sector.

- The first public sector unit was "Vishveshvaraya Iron and Steel works" at Bhadrawati.

Public Sector Steel Plants

Location	Assistance
Rourkela (Odisha)	Germany
Bhilai (Chhattisgarh)	Russia
Durgapur (WB)	UK
Bokaro (Jharkhand)	Russia
Burnpur (WB)	Acquired from private sector in 1976
Vishakhapatnam (AP)	Russia
Salem (Tamil Nadu)	Government of India (No external assistance)
Vijayanagara (Karnataka)	Government of India
Bhadrawati (Karnataka)	Nationalisation of Vishveshvaraya Iron and Steel Ltd. (owned by Centre and State Government)

Jute industry is an important industry for a country like India, because not only it earns foreign exchange but also provides substantial employment opportunities in agriculture and industrial sectors.

- Its first modernised industrial unit was established at Reshra in West Bengal in 1855.
- The jute industry in the country is traditionally export oriented. India ranks number one in the raw jute and jute goods production and number two in export of jute goods in the world.

Cotton and Textile Industry

- Oldest industry of India, and employs largest number of workers.
- The first Indian modernised cotton cloth mill was established in 1818 at Fort Gloaster near Calcutta. But this mill was not successful.
- The second mill named "Mumbai's Spinning and Weaving Co." was established in 1854 at Bombay by KGN Daber.

Sugar industry is the second largest industry among agriculture-based industries in India.

- India is now one of the largest producer and consumer of sugar in the world.
- Maharashtra contributes over one third of the Indian total sugar output, followed closely by Uttar Pradesh.

Paper Industry

- The first mechanised paper mill was set up in 1812 at Serampur in West Bengal.
- The paper industry in India is ranked among the 15 top global paper industries.

Silk Industry

- India is the second-largest(first being China) country in the world in producing natural silk. At present, India produces about 16% silk of the world.
- India enjoys the distinction of being the only country producing all the five known commercial varieties of silk *viz* Mulberry, Tropical Tussar, Oak Tussar, Eri and Muga.

Petroleum and Natural Gas

- First successful Oilwell was dug in India in 1889 at Digboi, Assam.
- At present a number of regions with oil reserves have been identified and oil is being extracted in these regions.
- For exploration purpose, Oil and Natural Gas Commission (ONGC) was established in 1956 at Dehradun, Uttarakhand.

08

Money and Banking

(SOURCES)

Class-IX & X Old NCERT Chap 3 (The Infrastructure of the Indian Economy), Chap 5 (The State and Economic Development), Class-X New NCERT Chap 3 (Money and Credit), Class-XII New NCERT Chap 3 (Money and Banking), Class-XII Old NCERT Chap 7 (Money and Banking System Appendix) Tamil Nadu Board (Class-XII), NIOS

Introduction

- Money and banking are the cornerstones of a strong and effective economic and financial system. Both money and banking have evolved over centuries.
- In past times, there was no concept of money and people simply exchanged commodities with each other i.e. through barter system.
- Exchange of commodities without mediation of money is called **Barter exchange**. There were many issues with barter exchanges like Double coincidence of want, difficult to carry forward wealth and absence of a standard unit of account. Therefore, it became essential to accept a common medium of exchange i.e. money.

Money

- Money is the most commonly accepted medium of exchange, any object which is generally accepted as means of payment is money. Currency, in the form of notes or coins, is one type of money.

Purchasing Power of Money

The value of a currency expressed in terms of the number of goods and services that one unit of money can buy, is referred to as purchased power of money.

It can be categorised into following two parts :

(i) **Domestic Purchasing Power** Such purchasing power under by which goods are purchased within the territories of a nation, is termed as Domestic Purchasing Power.

(ii) **International Purchasing Power** Such domestic purchasing power by which goods and services are purchased from another nation is termed as International Purchasing Power.

Types of Money

The types of money circulated in an economy are as follows:

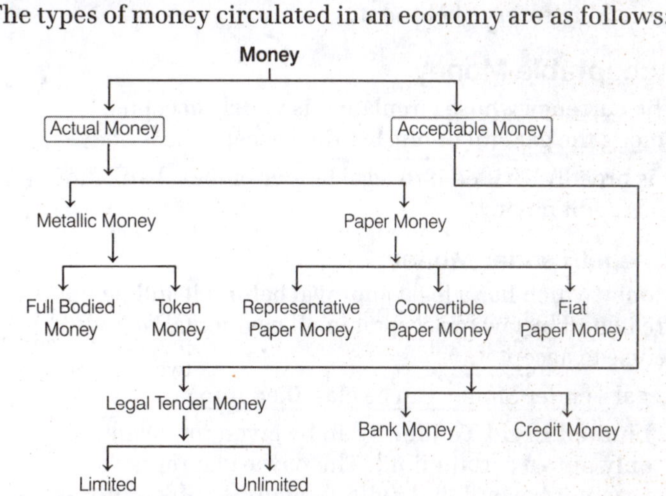

Actual Money

Money, which actually circulates in the economy in terms of, which all payments are made and general purchasing power is held as a medium of exchange.

Actual money is divided into two types :

1. Metallic Money

It is made of metal such as gold and silver. Coins of all denominations circulating in the economy are examples of metallic money. Metallic money is classified into two categories :

- **Full-bodied Money** If the face value of money is equal to its value as a commodity, it is called full-bodied money. If a gold coin of face value ₹ 100/- contains gold worth of ₹ 100/- it will be called full bodied money or sometimes standard money.
- **Token Money** If the face value of money is more than its value as commodity or intrinsic value it is known as token money.

2. Paper Money

Money made of paper is called paper money. It includes different denominations. Paper money is further classified into following forms :

- **Representative Paper Money** If paper is issued by keeping a 100% gold reserve of full-bodied coins or gold bullion, it will be called representative money.
- **Convertible Paper Money** If paper money can be converted into gold coins or gold bullion on demand, it is referred to as convertible money. This type of money is issued by keeping a metallic reserve of equal amount behind it.
- **Fiat or In-convertible Paper Money** Money which cannot be converted into full-bodied coins or gold bullion on demand is called Fiat or In-convertible paper money. It is usually issued without keeping metallic reserve behind it.

Acceptable Money

The currency whose circulation is widely accepted among the general public is called acceptable money.

It is broadly divided into legal tender money, bank money and credit money.

1. Legal Tender Money

Money which has a legal approval behind it and people are bound by law to accept it in all payments. Nobody can refuse to accept it.

Legal Tender Money can be classified into :

- **Limited Legal Tender** It can be given in payments only upto a certain limit. The payee can refuse to accept it beyond that limit. In many Asian countries, 25 paise coins and coins of low denominations are limited legal tender. The coins in India are also considered as limited legal tender. These coins can be given as payments up to ₹ 1000 only.
- **Unlimited Legal Tender** Unlimited legal tender means that money, which can be given in payments upto any limit.

2. Bank Money

Currency which is operated by banks, post offices and other financial institutions is called banking currency or money. It can be classified into following forms:

- **Cheque** It is provided by banks to account holders. Through this, a person can transfer money from his account to the other person account without using physical money.
- **Demand Draft** It is a pre-payment tool, issued by banks after collecting the amount and commission. It can be issued in the name of individual or entity and it can be received only at a particular branch of a particular city.
- **Travellers Cheque** It is a cheque on which applicants signature is on the front page, the payment of cheque can be received from any branch of the concerned bank in the country.
- **Postal Order** Money can be sent by post through this system. It can be purchased at a post office and is payable at another post office to the named recipient. In return, a fee for service is paid by the purchaser to the post office.

3. Credit Money

Credit currency means the currency in which the credit is denominated, provided that financing agreement between the two parties.

It can be classified into :

- **Bill of Exchange** It is an instrument in writing containing an unconditional order, signed by the maker, directing a certain person to pay on demand or at fixed or determinable future time a certain sum of money.
- **Hundi** A financial instrument developed in Medieval India for use in trade and credit transaction. It is an unconditional order in writing made by a person directing another to pay certain sum of money to a person named in the order.

Classification of Money on the Basis of Money Supply

- The total stock of money in circulation among the public at a particular point of time is called money supply. The measures of money supply in India are classified into four categories: M1, M2, M3 and M4 along with M0.

- This classification was introduced in April, 1977 by the Reserve Bank of India (RBI) as follows :
  - **Reserve Money** (M0) Currency in Circulation + Bankers' Deposits with RBI + Other deposits with RBI. It is also known as High-Powered Money, monetary base, base money, etc. It is the monetary base of the economy.
  - **Narrow Money** (M1) Currency with public + Demand Deposits with the Banking System (current account, saving account) + Other Deposits with RBI. M2 = M1 + Savings Deposits of Post Office Savings Banks.
  - **Broad Money** (M3) M1 + Time Deposits with the Banking System.

    M4 = M3 + All Deposits with Post Office Savings Banks.

Functions of Money

Various functions of money are as follows :

- **It acts as a medium of exchange** Any commodity can be bought through money.
- **A common measure of value** All commodities have their value that is expressed in terms of money.
- **Store of value acts as a standard for deferred payments** Future monetary obligations can be settled using money. For example, a loan, which is taken today is settled in installments.

Banking System

- A bank is a financial institution, which performs the deposit and lending function. A bank allows a person with excess money (saver) to deposit his money in the bank and earns an interest rate.
- The bank lends to a person who needs money (investor/ borrower) at an interest rate. Thus, the banks act as an intermediary between the saver and the borrower.
- The bank usually takes deposit from the public at a much lower rate called deposit rate and lends the money to the borrower at a higher interest rate called lending rate.
- The difference between the deposit and lending rate is called 'net interest spread' and the interest spread constitutes the bank's income.
- The important functions of a bank are as follows :
  - Accepting deposits
  - Lending money
  - Financial intermediation
  - Easy payment and withdrawals
  - Risk management
  - Economic development

Types of Deposits Held by a Bank

The various types of deposits held by a bank are as follows :

- **Demand Deposits** This money can be withdrawn at any time (on-demand) from the bank. These deposits are 100% liquid. These deposits include :
  - Current account
  - The demand liability portion of a saving account
- **Time Deposits** Money can be withdrawn only after maturity or with a penalty before maturity. These includes :
  - Fixed deposits
  - Recurring deposits
  - Time liability of saving account
- **Other Deposits** Demand Deposits with RBI, which includes demand deposits of public financial institutions, demand deposits of foreign central banks and international financial institutions like IMF, World Bank, etc.

Development of Banking System in India

- The first bank to be established in India was **Bank of Hindustan** in the year 1770 in Calcutta. This bank was completely based on **European Banking System**.
- For the benefits of East India Company, Bank of Bengal in 1806, Bank of Bombay in 1840 and Bank of Madras in 1843 were established. In 1921, these three banks were merged to form **Imperial Bank of India**.
- In 1894, **Punjab National Bank** was established. This was the first bank to be completely established and run by Indians.
- In 1934, **Indian Reserve Bank Act** was passed by Central Banking Investigation Committee. As a result, **Reserve Bank of India** started functioning on 1st April, 1935.
- Period of 1939-1946 is referred to as duration of **Banking Expansion in India**.
- On 1st January, 1949, **Reserve Bank of India** was nationalised.
- On 1st July, 1955, **Imperial Bank of India** was nationalised and renamed as the **State Bank of India**.
- After implementation of New Economic Policy, foreign banks were allowed to open their branches in India.

Types of Banks in India

There are various types of banks in India such as Central bank, Cooperative banks, Commercial banks, Local Area banks, Regional Rural banks, Specialised banks, Small Finance banks, Payments banks, etc.

Central Bank

- Each country has a Central bank that looks after all of the country's other financial institutions. Our country's Central bank is the **Reserve Bank of India**.
- The Central bank's principal role is to serve as the government's bank and to oversee and regulate the country's other banking institutions.
- The functions of a country's Central bank are listed below:
  - Assisting other financial institutions.
  - Issuing money and enforcing monetary policies.
  - Supervising of the financial systems.
- In other words, the country's Central bank is also known as the banker's bank because it assists other banks in the country and runs the country's financial system under the supervision of the Government.

Commercial Banks

- All banks which are mentioned in the Second Schedule of RBI Act, 1934 are known as **Scheduled Banks**. These banks comprise Scheduled Commercial Banks and Scheduled Cooperative Banks.
- Scheduled Commercial Banks in India are categorised into five different groups according to their ownership and/or nature of operation.
- Apart from basic banking business, banks also undertake other services such as safe custody of valuables, granting and issuance of letters of credit to facilitate International Trade, buying and selling in foreign exchange and collection of bills among others.
- Banks also act as agent of the government and other entities to undertake agency business.
- Extending loans and advances to the needy sectors of the economy on a priority basis is a very crucial function of the banking sector. Advances, deposits, money at call and short notice etc., is included in the assets of a Commercial Bank in India.
- The first bank of limited liability managed by Indians was **Oudh Commercial Bank** founded in 1881. Subsequently, Punjab National Bank was established in 1894.
- Swadeshi Movement, which began in 1906, encouraged the formation of a number of commercial banks.
- These bank's primary source of funds is public deposits. Commercial banks can be public sector banks, private sector banks and foreign banks.
  - **Public sector banks** are those in which, the government or the country's central bank owns the majority of the stock.
  - Banks in the **private sector** are those in which a private entity, an individual, or a group of people owns the majority of the stock.
  - **Foreign banks** category includes banks with headquarters in other nations and branches in India.

Classification of Commercial Banks

There are two types of commercial banks :

Scheduled Commercial Banks

- Scheduled Commercial Banks in India are those banks which have been included in the Second Schedule of **Reserve Bank of India** (RBI) **Act, 1934**.
- Reserve Bank of India (RBI) in turn includes only those banks in this schedule which satisfy the criteria mentioned in Section 42(6) (a) of the Reserve Bank of India Act, 1934.
- Criteria for scheduled bank are:
  - Scheduled banks are those banks whose minimum paid up capital and reserve amount is upto ₹ 5 lakh.
  - These banks have to submit details of their activities to the Reserve Bank of India every week.

Non-Scheduled Commercial Banks

- Non-scheduled Commercial Banks are those which have not been included in the Second Schedule of the RBI Act, 1934. Non-scheduled banks are also subject to the statutory cash reserve requirement. But they are not required to keep them with the RBI; they may keep these balances with themselves.
- They are not entitled to borrow from the RBI for normal banking purposes, though they may approach the RBI for accommodation under abnormal circumstances.

Cooperative Banks

- These banks are governed by a law enacted by the State Government. They provide short-term loans to agriculture and related industries.
- Cooperative bank's principal purpose is to enhance social welfare by providing low-interest loans.
- They are arranged in a **three-tier system :**
  - State Cooperative Banks, **Tier 1** (State Level) (regulated by RBI, State Government, NABARD)
  - Central/District Cooperative Banks, **Tier 2** (District Level)
  - **Tier 3** (Village Level) – Agriculture (Primary) Cooperative Banks

Local Area Banks (LAB)

- These banks were introduced in India in 1906 with the purpose of enabling the local institutions to pool and mobilise the rural savings.
- These banks are governed by the **Companies Act, 1956.**

Regional Rural Banks (RRB)

- Operating under the Regional Rural Bank, Act of 1976, these banks started in 1975. The establishment of 196 RRBs took place in between 1987 – 2005.

- These banks aim at the development of rural and agricultural areas with the help of concessional loan offerings.
- The ownership of these banks belong 50% to the national government, 15% to the State Government and 35% to the sponsored commercial bank.
- From 2005 onwards, the merging of these banks by the government took place due to which the number was reduced to 86.

Specialised Banks

Certain banks exist just to serve a certain purpose. Specialised banks are the name for several types of financial institutions. These are classified as :

- **Micro Units Development and Refinance Agency Bank** (MUDRA Bank) It is a public sector financial institution in India. It provides loans at low rates to micro-finance institutions and non-banking financial institutions, which then provide credit to MSMEs.
- **SIDBI** (Small Industries Development Bank of India) SIDBI can provide loan for a small scale enterprise or business. With the support of this bank, small businesses can get current technology and equipment.
- **Export and Import Bank** (EXIM Bank) EXIM Bank stands for Export and Import Bank. This type of bank can provide loans or other financial help to foreign countries that are exporting or importing goods.
- **NABARD** (National Bank for Agricultural and Rural Development) People can resort to NABARD for any type of financial support for rural, handicraft, village and agricultural development.

Small Finance Banks

- As the name implies, this type of bank, provides loans and financial help to micro industries, small farmers and the unorganised sector of society.
- The country's Central bank oversees these institutions, e.g., Ujjivan Small Finance Bank.

Payments Banks

- The Reserve Bank of India conceptualised the payments bank, a newly developed form of banking.
- People who have a payment bank account can only deposit upto ₹ 1,00,000 and cannot apply for loans or credit cards through this account.
- Payment banks provide services such as internet banking, mobile banking and debit card issuance. E.g., Paytm Post Payments Bank.

Nationalisation of Banks

- From 1st February, 1969, the government imposed social control on banks by introducing certain provisions in the **Banking Regulation Act, 1949.**
- Then, all those banks which were taken over through Banking Companies Bill are called nationalised banks.
- Government of India issued an ordinance in 1969 and nationalised **14 largest commercial banks** in India from the midnight of 19th July, 1969. On 15th April, 1980, six more banks having demand and time liabilities of not less than ₹ 200 crore were nationalised.
- The undertakings of these banks are taken over and vested in six corresponding new banks under the **Banking Companies** (Acquisition and Transfer of Undertakings) **Act**, 1980.
- Later on, in the year 1993, the government merged New Bank of India with Punjab National Bank. It was the only merger between nationalised banks and resulted in the reduction of the number of nationalised banks from 20 to 19.

Merging of SBI and Mahila Bank

- **State Bank of India** (SBI) was previously called Imperial Bank of India in 1921, which was created by amalgamation of 3 Presidency Banks *viz*, Bank of Bengal, Bank of Bombay and Bank of Madras. It was nationalised in 1955.
- **Bharatiya Mahila Bank** (BMB) was created and incorporated through an Act of Parliament in Mumbai on 19th November, 2013. This was the only and first public sector bank incorporated through an Act of Parliament.
- State Bank of India, merged five of its Associate Banks and Bharatiya Mahila Bank with itself on 1st April, 2017. With the merger, SBI became one of the top 50 global banks.

Merger of Other Banks

- The **Bank of Baroda** was founded by Maharaja of Baroda, Maharaja Sayajirao Gaekwad III on 20th July, 1908. It was nationalised on 19th July, 1969 by the Government of India.
- **Vijaya Bank** and **Dena Bank** merged with Bank of Baroda (BoB) on 1st April, 2019. This merger has created BoB as the third largest public sector bank of India.
- Government has merged Indian Bank with Allahabad Bank, Oriental Bank of Commerce (OBC) and United Bank of India with Punjab National Bank, Syndicate Bank with Canara Bank and Andhra Bank with Union Bank of India on 1st April, 2020. After merger, there are only 12 Public Sector Banks of India.

Reserve Bank of India (RBI)

- The RBI is the supreme monetary and banking authority in the country and controls the banking system in India.
- It is called the 'Reserve Bank' as it keeps the reserves of all commercial banks. Before the establishment of RBI, the functions of a Central Bank were virtually done by the **Imperial Bank of India**.
- RBI started its operations from 1st April, 1935. It was established *via* the RBI Act 1934, that's why it is a statutory body. Similarly, SBI is also a statutory body deriving its legality from SBI Act, 1955.
- RBI did not start as a Government-owned bank but as a **private-owned bank**.
- After the independence, the Government passed Reserve Bank (Transfer to Public Ownership) Act, 1948 and took over RBI from private shareholders after paying appropriate compensation.
- **Nationalisation of RBI** took place in 1949 and from 1st January, 1949, RBI started working as a government-owned bank.
- Original headquarters of RBI was in Kolkata, but in 1937, it was shifted to **Mumbai.**

Functions of the RBI

The functions of RBI are as follows :

- **Bank of Issue** Issuing money is the exclusive right of RBI. All notes except ₹ 1 note and coins are issued by the RBI. ₹ 1 notes and coins are issued by the Ministry of Finance and circulated by RBI.
- **Custodian and Manager of Foreign Exchange** It keeps the foreign exchange (i.e. foreign currency) which flows into the country. It also keeps the foreign exchange rate stable to a certain extent.
- **Banker and Debt Manager to Government** It acts as a banker to both Central and State Governments. It keeps deposits of government and lend to government.
- **Banker to Bank** It is the banker of all the banks. It keeps the reserve of the banks like Cash Reserve Ratio (CRR) with it. It provides financial assistance to banks against mortgaged securities. Usually banks borrow and lend money among themselves *via* call money market, regulated by RBI.
- **Monetary Management** Controller of money supply, makes monetary policy, control credit etc.
- **Financial Regulator** It is financial regulator for Commercial banks, Credit information companies, Regional Rural Banks (RRBs), Local Area Banks, Non-Banking Financial Company (NBFC) etc.
- **Representative Role** RBI represents the Government as a member of the International Monetary Fund (IMF) and World Bank.
- **Central Clearance and Accounts Settlement** As RBI keeps cash reserves from commercial banks therefore it rediscounts their bills of exchange easily.
- **Developmental Role** Performing a variety of developmental and promotional functions under which it set up institutions like Industrial Development Bank (IDBI), Small Industries Development Bank (SIDBI), etc.
- **Promotional Roles** Consumer protection, Ombudsman, Financial Inclusion through Priority Sector Lending (PSL) norms, 25% rural branch requirements etc., are some of the promotional roles played by the RBI.

Sources of Income and Expenditure of RBI

Income	Expenditure
Returns from foreign currency assets.	Expenditure on printing of currency.
Interest on rupee-denominated government bonds.	Expenditure on staff.
Interest on overnight lending to Commercial banks.	Commission given to Commercial banks.
Management commission on handling the borrowings of Central and State Governments.	Commission given to primary dealers.

Monetary Policy of RBI

Monetary Policy is an instrument under RBI, aimed at regulating interest rates, money supply and availability of credit in an economy. RBI decides monetary policy cycle on bi-monthly basis.

Various objectives of Monetary Policy are as follows :

- **Economic and financial stability** To regulate monetary expansion so as to maintain a reasonable degree of price stability.
- **Development** To ensure adequate financial resources for the purpose of development.
- **Flow of credit** To provide adequate flow of credit to productive sectors.
- **Employment and growth** Promotion of productive investments and trade. Equitable distribution of income. Employment generation.
- **International trade and exports** Promotion of exports and economic growth. Maintaining exchange rate stability.

Tools of Monetary Policy

- **Quantitative tools** of monetary policy include Liquidity Adjustment Facility (Repo and Reverse Repo), Open Market Operations, SLR and CRR, Bank Rate, Credit Ceiling, Marginal Standing Facility.
- **Qualitative tools** of monetary policy include Credit Rationing, Moral Suasion, Prompt Corrective Action(PCA), Direct action by RBI on banks and Differential Interests Rates.

Quantitative Instruments of Monetary Policy

The quantitative instruments of monetary policy are as follows :

1. Cash Reserve Ratio (CRR)

- It is the certain percentage (fixed by the RBI) of Net Time and Demand Deposits of a Scheduled Bank in India, need to be kept with the RBI in the form of cash only. It aims to have control over banks credit.
- The ratio between 3% (floor) -15% (ceiling) is removed via **RBI** (Amendment) **Bill 2006.**
- An increase in CRR - higher proportion of deposits to be kept with RBI by banks - less funds are available to be provided as credit to the economy, money supply will decrease.

2. Statutory Liquidity Ratio (SLR)

- The Scheduled banks need to keep certain percentage (fixed by the RBI) of their Net Time and Demand Deposits kept with themselves (i.e. not with RBI) in the form of liquid assets such as cash, gold and selected government securities.
- Need of SLR is to prevent banks from lending all its deposits, which is too risky and it is mandatory under Banking Regulation Act 1949.
- Similar to CRR, SLR aimed to have control over banks credit.
- It includes **G-Secs,** thus it ensures a certain amount of money is secured for the government.
- There were excessively high rates (about 25-30%) prevalent before 1991 reforms with provision of ceiling and floor.
- An increase in SLR - higher proportion of funds to be kept aside by banks in liquid form - less funds available to be provided as credit to the economy - money supply will decrease.
- Higher the CRR and SLR, lower will be the liquidity in the system as banks will have lesser money for providing loans.
- For instance, the CRR and SLR rate is 4% and 19.5% respectively. Bank deposits are ₹ 100 crores then banks can sanction loans upto ₹ 76.5 crores.

3. Bank Rate

- Rate at which RBI provides long-term borrowings to its clients. Its clients include Central Government, State Governments, banks, financial institutions, cooperative banks etc.
- An increase in the bank rate symbolises tightening of RBI monetary policy (i.e. Dearer Monetary Policy).
- An increase in bank rate will make borrowing from RBI expensive - discourage banks from borrowing from RBI - money supply will tend to decrease.
- Presently, it is used as a penalty rate imposed by RBI on banks for violations of RBI directives.

4. Repo Rate (Policy Rate)

- It is the rate (Rate of Repurchase) at, which Commercial banks borrow from RBI (which provides short-term liquidity to banks) by mortgaging their dated **Government securities and Treasury** bills (T-Bills).
- Reduction in Repo rate helps the banks to get money at a cheaper rate and increase in Repo rate discourages the banks to borrow from RBI.
- The **Call Money Market of India** (inter-bank market) operates at this rate and banks use this route for overnight borrowings.
- Repo rate has direct relation with the interest rates banks charge on the loans they offer (as it affects the operational cost of the banks).

5. Reverse Repo Rate

- It is the rate at which RBI borrows from Commercial banks by mortgaging its dated Government securities and Treasury bills. An increase in Reverse Repo rate means that Commercial banks will get more incentives to park their funds with the RBI, thereby decreasing the supply of money in the market.
- A decrease in Reverse Repo rate means that Commercial banks will get less incentive to park their funds with RBI and thus more money is available in the market increasing the money supply.
- It has a direct bearing on the interest rates charged by the banks and the financial institutions on their different forms of loans.

6. Marginal Standing Facility (MSF)

- It was introduced to deal with unforeseen liquidity crunch because under **Liquidity Adjustment Facility** (LAF) banks can borrow overnight liquidity only by pledging securities over and above the securities held under SLR requirement.
- Liquidity management window given by RBI under, which banks can borrow additional overnight (one day) liquidity over and above LAF window.
- The interest rate for MSF is Repo rate + 1%. Usually, the Reverse Repo rate is Repo rate – 1%.
- Therefore, the Repo rate acts as an anchor rate. The Repo rate stands in the middle of two. The MSF rate stands above and Reverse Repo rate stands below the Repo rate.
- Under this facility, banks can borrow funds up to 1% of their **Net Demand and Time Liabilities** (NDTL).
- NDTL shows the difference between the sum of demand and time liabilities (deposits) of a bank (with the public or the other bank) and the deposits in the form of assets held by the other bank.

Bank's NDTL = Demand and Time Liabilities
– Deposits with other Banks

Open Market Operations (OMO)

- OMO refers to sale and purchase of government securities by RBI in the open market with the aim of influencing liquidity in the economy in the medium term.
- If the RBI sells these instruments, banks and the public will buy it and pay money to the RBI.
- If the RBI buys these instruments from instrument holders, it will pay money to the latter.
- During inflation, the RBI sells government securities. As a result money supply in the economy falls causing prices to fall.
- During deflation, the RBI will buy back the securities thus causing money supply to rise, which cures deficiency in demand.

Liquidity Adjustment Facilities (LAF)

- Monetary policy instrument that the RBI uses in order to influence the liquidity conditions in the market in the short-term. Under the LAF window, the RBI uses various instruments to inject or absorb liquidity to or from the market respectively.
- Repo and Reverse Repo rates are a part of RBI's **Liquidity Adjustment Facility (LAF).**
- The RBI introduced LAF as a result of the **Narasimham Committee** on Banking Sector Reforms (1998).

Long-Term Repo Operations (LTRO)

- New policy tool used by the RBI to inject more liquidity into the economy similar to the term Repos, but with a longer maturity period of 1 year and 3 years.
- Through the LTRO, the RBI seeks to inject long- term liquidity into the economy at a lower interest rate.
- The LTROs would be carried out through e-Kuber. e-Kuber is the Core Banking Solution (CBS) of the RBI, which enables each bank to connect their single current account across the country.

Qualitative Instruments of Monetary Policy

The qualitative instruments of monetary policy are as follows :

Credit Rationing

- It is a method by which the RBI seeks to limit the maximum amount of loans and advances.
- In certain cases, it also fix ceilings for specific categories of loans and advances.

Margin Requirements

- Qualitative tool used by the RBI in order to regulate the credit flow to a particular sector.
- When a bank advances credit to its customers it does so against collateral.
- However, there is a difference between the value of the security and the loan offered. This difference is called 'Margin'.

Moral Suasion

- It refers to a method adopted by the Central Bank to persuade or convince the Commercial banks to advance credit in the economic interest of the country.
- Since, it involves no administrative compulsion or threats of punitive action, it is a psychological and informal means of selective credit control.

Differential Rate of Interest (DRI)

- It is a lending programme launched by the government in April, 1972.
- It makes obligatory for all the public sector banks in India to lend 1% of the total lending of the preceding year to 'the poorest among the poor' at an interest rate of 4% per annum.

Direct Action

- This step is taken by the RBI against banks that don't fulfill conditions and requirements. RBI may refuse to rediscount their papers or may give excess credits or charge a penal rate of interest over and above the Bank rate, for credit demanded beyond a limit.

Prompt Corrective Action (PCA)

- The PCA is triggered when banks breach certain regulatory requirements like minimum capital and quantum of non-performing assets.
- To ensure that banks don't go bust, RBI has put in place some trigger points to assess, monitor, control and take corrective actions on banks, which are weak and troubled.

Consumer Credit Regulation

- In 1968, the Consumer Credit Protection Act, was passed to regulate the Consumer Credit Industry.
- It is designed to check the flow of credit for Consumer Durable Goods.

Monetary Policy Committee

- The Monetary Policy Committee (MPC) is a statutory and institutionalised framework under **the Reserve Bank of India Act, 1934**, for maintaining price stability, while keeping in mind the objective of growth.
- An RBI-appointed committee led by the then Deputy Governor Urjit Patel in 2014 recommended the establishment of the Monetary Policy Committee.
- The Governor of RBI is ex-officio Chairman of the committee. The committee comprises **six members** (including the Chairman) - three officials of the RBI and three external members nominated by the Government of India.
- Its all decisions are taken by majority with the Governor having the casting vote in case of a tie.
- The MPC determines the policy interest rate (Repo rate) required to achieve the Inflation target (4%).

- Inflation refers to the rise in the prices of most goods and services of daily or common use, such as food, clothing, housing, recreation, transport, consumer staples, etc.
- Inflation measures the average price change in a basket of commodities and services over time.
- Inflation is indicative of the decrease in the purchasing power of a unit of a country's currency. This could ultimately lead to a deceleration in economic growth. However, a moderate level of inflation is required in the economy to ensure that production is promoted.

Types of Inflation

The various types of inflation are discussed below :

Based on the Rate of Rising in Inflation

- **Creeping Inflation** Price rises at a very small rate (< 3 %). It is considered safe and essential for the economy.
- **Walking or Trotting Inflation** Price rises at moderate rate (3 % < Inflation < 10 %). Inflation at this rate is a warning signal for the economy.
- **Running Inflation** Price rises at high rate (10 % < Inflation < 20 %). It affects the economy adversely.
- **Hyperinflation or Galloping Inflation or Runway Inflation** Prices rise at a very high rate (20 % < Inflation < 100 %) and sometimes more than 100%. Hyperinflation brings the total collapse of the Economy. **e.g.,** Venezuela (9900%), Zimbabwe (670%), Sudan (76%) etc.

Based on the Causes

- **Demand Pull Inflation** When inflation arises due to higher demand for goods and services over the limited supply.
- **Cost-Push Inflation** When inflation arises due to higher input cost (for example, raw material, wages etc.) for goods and services over the limited supply.

Effects of Inflation

Effects of inflation are as follows :

- **Redistribution of Income and Wealth** Due to the effect of inflation, some group of people loses and another group of people gain.
- **Effects on Production and Consumption** Due to inflation, the demand decreases, which curtails the production.
- People try to use fewer services, which lead to a decrease in consumption.
- **Unfavourable Balance of Payments** Export decreases and import increases from other countries, which lead to a decrease in the forex reserve.

Other Important Terms Associated with Inflation

- **Deflation** It is a decrease in the general price level of goods and services. In another way, deflation is negative inflation. When the overall price level decreases, it is called deflation.
- **Stagflation** It is a situation of slow economic growth and relatively high unemployment.
- **Disinflation** It is a situation when the rate of inflation is at a slower rate. For example, if the Inflation of last month was 4% and the rate of inflation in the current month is 3%.
- **Reflation** It is deliberate action of the government to increase the rate of inflation to redeem the economy from a deflationary situation.
- **Core Inflation** It is a measure of price rise in the economy excluding the price rise of some products whose price is volatile and temporary in nature.
- **Devaluation of Money** It is a deliberate downward adjustment to the value of a country's currency, relative to another currency, group of currencies or standard.

Measures to Control Inflation

Some important and effective measures to control inflation are:

Monetary Measures

- **Credit Contraction** It is used by the RBI to control credit.
- **Demonetisation of Currency** Inflation can be controlled by demonetise currency of higher denominations. It is adopted when there is abundance of black money in the country.
- **Issue of New Currency** Under this measure, one new note is exchanged for a number of notes of the old currency. The value of bank deposit is also fixed accordingly. It is adopted when there is excessive issue of notes and there is hyper inflation in the country.

Fiscal Measures

- **Increase in Direct Taxes** Due to the increase in direct taxes, people have less money available to them and low demand from them leads to a lower price.
- **Price Control** By fixing the maximum price limit by authorities.
- **Reduction in Unnecessary Expenditure** Inflation can be curbed by reducing expenditure on non-development activities.

- **Increase in Savings** By motivating people to save money can help in reducing inflation. This will reduce disposable income and personal consumption expenditure.
- **Surplus Budget** This measure helps to reduce inflation by collecting more revenues and spending less.
- **Public Debt** Inflation can be curbed by stopping repayment of public debt and postponing it to future till inflationary pressure is controlled in the economy.

Other Measures

- **Trade Measures** Maintain proper supply in the economy by export and import of goods and services.
- **Increasing Production** By increasing production of essential goods, inflation can be controlled.
- **Rational Wage Policy** Under hyperinflation, there is a wage-price spiral. To control this, the government adopts a rational wage and income policy by freezing wages, incomes, profits, dividends, bonus, etc.
- **Rationing** It also helps to control inflation by distributing consumption of scarce goods to large number of consumers. It helps to stabilise the prices of necessary goods and assure distributive justice.

Measures of Inflation

In India, inflation is primarily measured by two main indices WPI and CPI, which measure wholesale and retail-level price changes, respectively.

Wholesale Price Index (WPI)

- It measures the changes in the prices of goods sold and traded in bulk by wholesale businesses to other businesses.
- It is published by the Office of Economic Adviser, **Ministry of Commerce and Industry.**
- It is the most widely used inflation indicator in India.
- Major criticism for this index is that the general public does not buy products at wholesale price.
- The base year of All-India WPI has been revised from 2004-05 to 2011-12 in 2017.

Consumer Price Index (CPI)

- It measures price changes from the perspective of a retail buyer. It is released by the **National Statistical Office** (NSO).
- The CPI calculates the difference in the price of commodities and services such as food, medical care, education, electronics etc, which Indian consumers buy for use.
- The CPI has several sub-groups including food and beverages, fuel and light, housing and clothing, bedding and footwear.
- **Four types of CPI** are as follows :
  (i) CPI for Industrial Workers (IW)
  (ii) CPI for Agricultural Labourer (AL)
  (iii) CPI for Rural Labourer (RL)
  (iv) CPI (Rural/Urban/Combined)
- Of these, the first three are compiled by the Labour Bureau in the Ministry of Labour and Employment whereas fourth is compiled by the NSO in the Ministry of Statistics and Programme Implementation. The base year for CPI is 2012.
- The Monetary Policy Committee (MPC) uses CPI data to control inflation. In April 2014, the Reserve Bank of India (RBI) had adopted the CPI as its key measure of inflation.

Demonetisation

- Demonetisation of currency means discontinuity of the particular currency and replacing it with a new currency.
- In the current context ₹ 500 and ₹ 1000 denomination currency notes discontinued to be as a legal tender and new ₹ 200, ₹ 500 and ₹ 2000 currency notes were introduced.
- This step has been taken by the Government on 8th November, 2016. The Indian Government had demonetised bank notes on two prior occasions also, once in 1946 and other in 1978.
- The Centeral Bank, RBI on 19th may, 2023 with draw ₹ 2000 notes from circulation.

Banking Sector Reforms

Government of India have introduce many banking sector reforms from time to time. Some of these are as follows :

Goiporia Committee

- This committee was constituted in 1990 under the chairmanship of MN Goiporia. The committee was given the mandate of exploring and giving recommendations for improving customer service in the banks.
- On its recommendations, Banking Ombudsman Scheme was launched in 1995.

Narasimham Committee Report I, 1991

- For promoting the healthy development of the financial sector, the Narasimham Committee made recommendations first in 1991.
- **Recommendations** of Narasimham Committee are :
  - Establishment of 4 tier hierarchy for banking structure with 3 to 4 large banks (including SBI) at the top and at bottom rural banks engaged in agricultural activities.
  - The supervisory functions over banks and financial institutions can be assigned to a quasi-autonomous body sponsored by RBI.

- Proper classification of assets and full disclosure of accounts of banks and financial institutions.
- Setting up an asset reconstruction fund to take over a portion of the loan portfolio of banks whose recovery has become difficult.

Narasimham Committee Report II, 1998

It submitted its report to the Government in April, 1998 with the following recommendations :

- **Strengthening Banks in India** The Committee considered the stronger banking system in the context of the Current Account Convertibility (CAC). It thought that Indian banks must be capable of handling problems regarding domestic liquidity and exchange rate management in the light of CAC. Thus, it recommended the merger of strong banks, which will have a 'multiplier effect' on the industry.
- **Narrow Banking** For successful rehabilitation of public sector banks, this committee recommended 'Narrow Banking Concept'. According to it, weak banks allowed to place their funds only in the short-term and risk-free assets.
- **Capital Adequacy Ratio** In order to improve the inherent strength of the Indian banking system, the committee recommended that the Government should raise the prescribed capital adequacy norms.
- **Review of Banking Laws** The committee emphasised need for reviewing and amending main laws governing Indian Banking Industry like RBI Act, Banking Regulation Act, Bank Nationalisation Act, etc. This upgrade will bring them in line with the present needs of the banking sector in India.

Damodaran Committee

- This Committee was formed in 2011 under the chairmanship of former SEBI Chairman **M Damodaran.**
- It was set-up by the Central Bank to look into the issues of customer services and evaluate the existing system of grievance redressal mechanism prevalent in banks, its structure and efficacy and recommend measures for expeditious resolution of complaints.

Usha Thorat Committee

- Reserve Bank of India (RBI) panel headed by **Usha Thorat,** Director of Centre for Advanced Financial Research and Learning (CAFRAL) on 29th August, 2011 presented its suggestion on Non-banking Finance Company (NBFC).
- It has **recommended** :
  - a higher capital norm of 12% for NBFCs;
  - asset classification and provisioning on the lines of banks;
  - more capital to be set aside by non-banking firms which are not sponsored by banks for capital market related and real estate lending;
  - a minimum asset size of over ₹ 50 crore for registering a new NBFC.

MV Nair Committee

- The Reserve Bank had constituted the Committee under the chairmanship of **Shri M V Nair** on 25th August, 2011 pursuant to the announcement made in the Monetary Policy Statement 2011-12.
- The Committee was to re-examine the existing classification and suggest revised guidelines with regard to priority sector lending and related issues.

Urjit Patel Committee

- Reserve Bank of India constituted **Urjit Patel Committee** on 12th September, 2013 to review and strengthen the monetary policy framework.
- This committee submitted its report in January 2014 to the then Governor.
- It suggested to keep **Consumer Price Index** under Monetary Policy.

Nachiket Mor Committee

- The Committee on Comprehensive Financial Services for Small Businesses and Low-Income Households was set up by the RBI in September 2013.
- This committee is commonly known as **Nachiket Mor Committee.**
- This committee was mandated with the task of framing a clear and detailed vision for financial inclusion and financial deepening in India.
- The **Wholesale Consumer Banks** and **Wholesale Investment Banks** would not take retail deposits but would instead focus their attention on expanding the penetration of credit services.
- The committee has suggested a fixed term of 5 years for the Chairman/Managing Director of a bank and a term of 3 years for a whole-time director.

PJ Nayak Committee

- The PJ Nayak Committee or officially the Committee to Review Governance of Boards of Banks in India was set up by the Reserve Bank of India (RBI) in January, 2014.
- Various **recommendations** related to PJ Nayak Committee are :
  - Repeal the Bank Nationalisation Act (1970, 1980), the SBI Act and SBI Subsidiaries Act. This is because these acts require the government to have above 50% share in the banks.
  - After the above acts are repealed, the government should set up a Bank Investment Company (BIC) as a holding company or a Core Investment Company (CIC). The government transfers its share in the banks to this BIC.

Thus, the BIC would become the parent holding company of all these national banks, which would become subsidiaries.

- As a result of this, all the PSBs (Public Sector Banks) would become 'limited' banks. BIC will be autonomous and have the power to appoint the Board of Directors and make other policy decisions.

Bimal Jalan Committee

- A committee, under the Chairmanship of former RBI Governor Bimal Jalan, was constituted to scrutinise the application for new banks in India.
- The Committee submitted its report in February 2014, recommending for the 'in-principle approval' of banking licenses to Bandhan Microfinance and IDFC (Infrastructure Development and Finance Corporation).

Basel Norms

- Basel norms or Basel accords are the international banking regulations issued by the Basel Committee on Banking Supervision.
- The Basel norms is an effort to coordinate banking regulations across the globe, with the goal of strengthening the international banking system.
- It is the set of the agreement by the Basel Committee of Banking Supervision, which focuses on the risks to banks and the financial system.
- The Basel Committee has issued three sets of regulations, which are known as **Basel-I, II** and **III.**
- **Basel-II norms** in India and overseas are yet to be fully implemented though India follows these norms.
- The deadline for the implementation of **Basel-III** was March, 2019 in India. It was postponed to March, 2020. In light of the coronavirus pandemic, the RBI decided to defer the implementation of Basel norms by further 6 months.

Governments Schemes/Organisations Associated with Banking

Some of the governments schemes/organisations associated with Banking are as follows :

New Bad Bank Structure

- The Union Cabinet approved ₹ 30,600 crore guarantee to back Security Receipts issued by **National Asset Reconstruction Company Limited** (NARCL) for acquiring stressed loan assets.
- The NARCL is a part of a New Bad Bank Structure that was announced in the Budget 2021. NARCL is registered as an Asset Reconstruction Company (ARC) under the SARFAESI Act. It has been established by banks to aggregate and consolidate stressed assets for their resolutions.

Bank Board Bureau

- The Bank Board Bureau was constituted on 28th February, 2016. The Bureau is mandated to play a critical role in reforming the troubled public sector banks by recommending appoint- ments to leadership positions (including Chairman of PSUs) and boards in banks and advise them on ways to raise funds and how to go ahead with mergers and acquisitions.
- **Vinod Rai**, former Comptroller and Auditor General of India, was named the first Chairman of the Banks Board Bureau. Currently, Bhanu Pratap Sharma is the new Chairman.

Financial Services Institution Bureau (FSIB)

- FSIB is established in place of the **Bank Board Bureau** (BBB) that will select the chiefs of the public sector banks and insurance companies.
- It have clear mandate to issue guidelines and select General Managers and the Directors of State run non-life insurers, general insurers and financial institutions.

Sovereign Gold Bond Scheme

- The Sovereign Gold Bond (SGB) scheme was launched by the Union Government on 22nd October, 2015. SGBs are government securities denominated in grams of gold.
- They are substitutes for holding physical gold. The bond is issued by Reserve Bank on behalf of Government of India. The Gold Bond Scheme, aimed at providing an alternative to buying physical gold, will offer investors a choice to buy bonds worth up to a maximum of 500 gm.
- These bonds will be issued in denominations of 5,10,50 and 100 grams of gold or other denominations.

MUDRA Bank

- Micro Units Development and Refinance Agency Bank (MUDRA Bank) was launched by Prime Minister Narendra Modi on 8th April, 2015 with a corpus of ₹ 20,000 crore and a credit guarantee corpus of ₹ 3,000 crore.
- It is a public sector financial institution in India. It provides loans at low rates to small entrepreneurs.
- MUDRA Bank was set-up through a statutory enactment. It will be responsible for developing and refinancing all Micro-Finance Institutions (MFIs) which are in the business of lending to micro and small business entities engaged in manufacturing, trading and service activities.
- The formation of the agency was initially announced in the 2015 Union Budget of India in February 2015.

Indradhanush Scheme, 2015

- The Public Sector Banks (PSBs) plays a vital role in Indian financial system.
- The assets quality of PSBs have deteriorated because of rising Non-Performing Assets (NPA). Indradhanush Scheme is for the banking reforms in India.

- The seven key reforms of Indradhanush mission include appointments, de-stressing capitalisation, empowerment, framework of accountability and governance reforms.

Financial Stability and Development Council (FSDC)

- FSDC is a non-statutory apex council under the Ministry of Finance constituted by the Executive Order in 2010. The **Raghuram Rajan Committee** (2008) on financial sector reforms first proposed the creation of FSDC.
- It is chaired by the Finance Minister and its members include the heads of all Financial Sector Regulators (RBI, SEBI, PFRDA and IRDA), Finance Secretary, Secretary of Department of Economic Affairs (DEA), Secretary of Department of Financial Services (DFS), and Chief Economic Adviser.

Banking Ombudsman Scheme

- This scheme was introduced in 1995. Presently, the Banking Ombudsman Scheme, 2006 is in operation.
- Its objective is to resolve complaints of customers of banks relating to certain services rendered by the banks. There are 22 regional offices of Banking Ombudsman in India.

Domestic Systemically Important Banks

- The Reserve Bank of India (RBI) has retained State Bank of India, ICICI Bank and HDFC Bank as Domestic Systemically Important Banks (D-SIBs) or banks that are considered as **'Too Big To Fail** (TBTF)'.
- Some banks, due to their size, cross-jurisdictional activities, complexity, lack of substitutability and interconnectedness, become systemically important.
- SIBs are perceived as banks that are **Too Big To Fail** (TBTF). This perception of TBTF creates an expectation of government support for these banks at the time of distress.

Non-Banking Financial Companies

- Non-Banking Financial Companies (NBFCs) are financial institutions that offer various banking services but do not have a banking licence.
- Generally, these institutions are not allowed to take traditional demand deposits–readily available funds, such as those in checking or savings accounts from the public. This limitation keeps them outside the scope of conventional oversight from federal and state financial regulators.
- NBFCs can offer banking services such as loans and credit facilities, currency exchange, retirement planning, money markets, underwriting and merger activities. NBFCs are officially classified under the 2010 Dodd- Frank Wall Street Reform and Consumer Protection Act.
- The Act describes them as companies whose more than 85% consolidated annual gross revenues or consolidated assets are financial in nature.
- This classification technically encompasses a wide range of companies offering bank-like financing and investing services. Examples of NBFCs include insurance companies, money market funds, asset managers, hedge funds, private equity firms, mobile payment systems, micro-lenders and peer-to-peer lenders.

Different Types/Categories of NBFCs Registered with RBI

Within the broad categorisation, the different types of NBFCs are as follows :

- Asset Finance Company (AFC)
- Investment Company (IC)
- Loan Company (LC)
- Infrastructure Finance Company (IFC)
- Systemically Important Core Investment Company (CIC-ND-SI)
- Infrastructure Debt Fund - Non-Banking Financial Company (IDF-NBFC)
- Non-Banking Financial Company - Micro Finance Institution (NBFC-MFI)
- Non-Banking Financial Company – Factors (NBFC-Factors)
- Mortgage Guarantee Companies (MGC)
- NBFC- Non-Operative Financial Holding Company (NOFHC)

Bitcoin and Cryptocurrency

- Bitcoin is a type of digital currency that enables instant payments to anyone.
- Bitcoin was introduced in 2009. Bitcoin is based on an open-source protocol and is not issued by any either one Central authority.
- A digital asset, which works as a medium of exchange wherein individual coin ownership records are stored in the form of a computerised database.
- **El Salvador** has become the first country to formally adopt bitcoin as legal tender.
- Strong cryptography is used to secure transaction records, to control creation of additional coins and to verify transfer of ownership of coins. It does not exist in physical form and is not issued by Central authority.

Extra Facts From Tamil Nadu Board and NIOS

- **Cryptocurrency** A digital currency in which encryption techniques are used to regulate the generation of units of currency and verify the transfer of funds, operating independently of a Central Bank.
- The **Riksbank**, which had sprung from a private bank established in 1656 is the oldest central bank in the world.
- The **first bank of India** was Bank of Hindustan (1770). The Bank of Bengal was established in 1809 and Bank of Bombay and Madras was established in 1840 and 1843 respectively. All three merged and rechristened as Imperial Bank of India in 1921. It was nationalised and renamed as SBI in 1955.
- **Primary functions of Commercial banks** are- Accepting deposits and advancing loans. The secondary functions of Commercial banks are- Agency services, General utility services, transfer of funds and credit creation.
- **Loans offered** are many times more than the deposits received by banks. This function of banks is known as 'Credit Creation'.
- **E-banking** also known as internet banking, is an electronic payment system that enables customers of a bank or other financial institution to conduct a range of financial transactions through the financial institution's website.

Difference between RTGS and NEFT

RTGS	NEFT
Real Time Gross Settlement	National Electronic Fund Transfer
Transactions happens in real time hence fast	Transactions happens in batches hence slow
Timings : 9:00 am to 4:30 pm (1:30 pm on Saturday)	Timings : 8:00 am to 6:30 pm (12: 30 pm on Saturday)
Minimum amount for RTGS transfer is ₹ 2 lakh	No minimum limit

- **ATMs** transformed the bank tech system when they were first introduced in 1967.
- A **Debit card** is a card allowing the holder to transfer money electronically from their bank account when making a purchase.
- A **Credit card** is a payment card issued to users (cardholders) to enable the cardholder to pay a merchant for goods and services based on the cardholder's promise to the card issuer to pay them for the amounts so paid plus the other agreed charges.
- Once the borrower fails to make interest or principal payments for 90 days the loan is considered to be a **Non- Performing Asset** (NPA).
- **Demonetisation** It is the act of stripping a currency unit of its status as legal tender. It occurs whenever there is a change of national currency.
- **Some Other Types of Inflation** (on the basis of inducement)
  - (i) **Currency Inflation** The excess supply of money in circulation causes rise in price level.
  - (ii) **Credit Inflation** When banks are liberal in lending credit, the money supply increases and thereby rising prices.
  - (iii) **Deficit Induced Inflation** The deficit budget is generally financed through printing of currency by the Central Bank. As a result, prices rise.
  - (iv) **Profit Induced Inflation** When the firms aim at higher profit, they fix the price with higher margin. So prices go up.
  - (v) **Scarcity Induced Inflation** Scarcity of goods happens either due to fall in production (e.g., farm goods) or due to hoarding and black marketing.
  - (vi) **Tax Induced Inflation** Increase in indirect taxes like excise duty, custom duty and sales tax may lead to rise in price (e.g., petrol and diesel). This is also called taxflation.

09

Public Finance, Fiscal Policy and Budget

[SOURCES]

Class-IX & X Old NCERT Chap 5 (The State and Economic Development), Class-XII New NCERT Chap 5 (Government Budget and the Economy), Class-XII Old NCERT Chap 8 (Economy and Government Budget)
Tamil Nadu Board (Class-XII), NIOS

Public Finance

- Public finance is the study of the role of the government in the economy.
- This is the management of a country's revenue, expenditures and debt load through various government and Quasi-government institutions.
- Public finance explores, the financial well-being of both the State Government and local bodies in India.

Division of Public Finance

Public finance is divided into Public Income and Public Expenditure

Public Income

All the financial resources of the Central Government are called Public finance. Under this, public income and all expenditure are included

Public income has following two parts

1. Revenue Receipts

- Those public receipts in which neither the government's contribution increases nor the government's assets decreases, they are called as revenue receipts.
- Revenue receipts has two sub-categories i.e., tax revenue and non-tax revenue.
  - **Tax revenue** includes taxes and duties imposed by the Federal government. In the budget, new taxes of the government, old taxes, rates, etc., are proposed to be amended or continued in their present form.
  - **Non-tax revenue** includes all other revenue receipts of the government. These include the prices of goods and services provided by the government on a commercial basis under commercial revenue.
- These include the prices of postal materials, all toll taxes from government authorities, interest on loans taken, receipts of electricity and railway services.
- Another sources of revenue on investments made by the government are accrued dividends and interests.

Following are the major sources of revenue:

(i) **Taxable income** It is an obligatory payment made by the public to the government, through which the government receives money for public expenditure. The income received from taxes is divided into two parts.

- **Direct tax** It is the tax which is collected from the person on whom it is levied i.e., it is directly levied on income tax. Income tax is the main direct tax.
- **Indirect tax** This is a tax that is collected through an intermediary. These taxes are levied on goods and services. Goods and Services Tax (GST) applicable from 1st July, 2017 is an adjustment of more than 17 indirect taxes.

(ii) **Profits and Dividends** The government receives profits and dividends every year from various types of companies like Steel Authority of India Limited, Oil and Natural Gas Corporation, etc.

(iii) **Interest Income** The Central Government gives loans to the State Government and other institutions, from which the Central Government receives income in the form of annual interest. Income received in the form of interest is an important formula for income from non-tax sources.

2. Capital Receipts

- Those receipts in return of which the government has to pay are called capital receipts. This payment is made in the coming financial year.
- The most prominent of these is the loan taken by the government from the public, which is named as market loan.
- Capital gains are also known as capital account and they are long-term in nature.

Public Expenditure

The entire public expenditure incurred by the government is divided into two parts :

1. Revenue Expenditure

- The expenditure which ordinarily does not constitute an asset is called Revenue expenditure.
- It is the expenditure of the Central Government for purpose other than the creation of physical or financial assets.
- It is related to governments general functioning of departments and miscellaneous services, debt conveyed by the government interest payment, grants made to State Government and other parties, etc. are incurred.
- In the budget document, the total revenue expenditure is divided into two parts:
  (i) **Planned Revenue Expenditure** This expenditure is called planned revenue expenditure, through this expenditure, production assets are created. It is related to various Economic Welfare Schemes. Central plans, central assistance for planning of States and Union Territories are included in this expenditure.
  (ii) **Non-Planned Revenue Expenditure** This revenue expenditure includes comprehensive expenditure on general economic and social services rendered. The main components of this expenditure are interest, payment, defence services, gratuity, salary and pension. No development work is done from this public expenditure, for this, money is arranged from the Consolidated Funds of India.

2. Capital Expenditure

- These are those expenditure of the government which result in physical or financial creation of assets or reduction of financial liabilities.
- Capital expenditure mainly consists of land, building, machinery, investments in plants and components.
- Under this head loans given by the Center to States, government companies and corporations and other institutions are also shown.
- These expenditures increase the assets of the government, these expenditures are productive, whose value keeps getting available for many years.

Fiscal Policy

- Fiscal policy refers to the use of government spending and tax policies to influence economic conditions, especially macro-economic conditions.
- It includes aggregate demand for goods and services, employment, inflation and economic growth.
- Fiscal policy is largely based on ideas from **John Maynard Keynes**, who argued governments could stabilise the business cycle and regulate economic output. Through fiscal policy, the government of a country controls the flow of tax revenues and public expenditure to navigate the economy. This is done by way of Government Budgeting.

Features of Fiscal Policy

The features of fiscal policy are as follows :

- Fiscal policy means measures by which a government adjusts its level of spending in order to monitor and influence the nation's economy.
- Fiscal policy is based on the theories of British economist **John Maynard Keynes.**
- The Keynesian theory, basically, states that government can influence macro-economic productivity levels by increasing or decreasing tax levels and public spending.
- It influence by the curbs inflation, increases employment and maintains healthy value of money.
- Fiscal policy also feeds into economic trends and influences Monetary policy.
- When the government receives more than it spends, it has a surplus. If the government spends more than it receives, it has a deficit.

Financial Deficit

A deficit is the amount by which a sum falls short of some reference amount. The meaning of deficit differs from that of debt, which is an accumulation of yearly deficits.

There are four types of financial deficit as follows :

1. Fiscal Deficit

- A more comprehensive indicator of the government's deficit is the fiscal deficit. This is the sum of revenue and capital expenditures less all revenue and capital receipts other than loans taken.
- This gives a more holistic view of the government's funding situation, since it gives the difference between all receipts and expenditures other than loans taken to meet such expenditures.

Fiscal Deficit = Revenue Receipts (Net tax revenue + Non-tax revenue) + Capital Receipts (only recoveries of loans and other receipts) – Total Expenditure (Plan and Non-plan)

There are three types of fiscal deficit as follows :

(i) Gross Fiscal Deficit

- The Gross Fiscal Deficit (GFD) of government is the excess of its total expenditure, current and capital, including loans net of recovery, over revenue receipts (including external grants) and non-debt capital receipts.

Gross Fiscal Deficit = Total Expenditure – (Revenue Receipts + Non-debt Creating Capital Receipts)

- Non-debt creating capital receipts are those receipts which are not borrowings and therefore, do not give rise to debt. Examples are recovery of loans and the proceeds from the sale of Public Sector Units (PSUs).

(ii) Net Fiscal Deficit

- The Net Fiscal Deficit is the **Gross Fiscal Deficit** (GFD) reduced by net lending by government.

(iii) Fiscal Imbalance and Deficit Financing

- Fiscal imbalance is a situation, in which there is a gap between revenue and expenditure.
- Deficit financing is a method of filling this gap which in India means borrowing from the RBI against the issue of Treasury Bills and running down of accumulated cash balances.

2. Revenue Deficit

It refers to an excess of government's revenue expenditure over the revenue receipts. It is expressed as

Revenue Deficit = Revenue Expenditure – Revenue Receipts

- This variable includes only those transactions that affect the current income and expenditure of the government.
- A higher revenue deficit implies that the government is using up its saved resources, due to a scarcity of the receipts.
- It is an undesirable situation as the government is forced to borrow for its regular consumption processes. This leads to additional burden of loans and liabilities on the government, which might force the government to cut its planned expenditure (because the non-planned expenditure cannot be curbed much).

3. Capital Deficit

- It refers to an unbalance in a nation's Balance of Payments capital account, in which payments made by the country for purchasing foreign assets exceed payments received by the country for selling domestic assets.
- In other words, investment by the domestic economy in foreign assets is less than foreign investment in domestic assets. This is generally not a desirable situation for a domestic economy.

Capital Deficit = Capital Receipts – Disbursement on Capital Account

Capital deficit can be divided into three parts which are as follows :

(i) Budget Deficit

- The amount by which a government, company or individual's spending exceeds its income over a particular period of time is known as budget deficit, also called deficit or deficit spending, opposite of budget surplus.

(ii) Primary Deficit

- The borrowing requirements of the government include interest obligations on accumulated debt. The primary deficit indicates the deficit amount that the government needs to borrow for consumption and investment purposes. Thus, primary deficit can be defined as

Primary Deficit = Gross Fiscal Deficit – Net Interest Liabilities

- The net liabilities consist of interest payments minus interest receipts by the government on net domestic lending.

(iii) Gross Primary Deficit

- It is the Gross Fiscal Deficit less interest payments while the primary revenue deficit is the revenue deficit less interest payments.

4. Monetary Losses

- Increment in net credit of RBI is monetary loss for the Central Government.

Monetary Losses = Net growth of holding of treasury bill of RBI + Contribution of RBI in market borrowing of Central Government

Government Budgeting

- Government budgeting in India is a comprehensive process involving the preparation, enactment and execution of budgets by the centre or states.
- As per the Article 112 of the Constitution of India, the Union Budget of a fiscal year refers to the '**Annual financial statement**' of the Union Government for that particular fiscal year.
- It contains a detailed account of the estimated receipts and expenditures of the government for a particular fiscal year that runs from 1st April to 31st March.
- In addition to it, the **Budget contains** :
  - Estimates of revenue and capital receipts
  - Ways and means to raise the revenue
  - Estimates of expenditure
  - Details of the actual receipts and expenditure of the closing financial year and the reasons for any deficit or surplus in that year
  - The economic and financial policy of the coming year, i.e., taxation proposals, prospects of revenue, spending programme and introduction of new schemes/projects.
- In Parliament, the Budget goes through following six stages:
  (i) Presentation of Budget
  (ii) General discussion
  (iii) Scrutiny by Departmental Committees
  (iv) Voting on Demands for Grants
  (v) Passing of Appropriation Bill
  (vi) Passing of Finance Bill
- The Budget Division of the Department of Economic Affairs in the Finance Ministry is the nodal body responsible for preparing the **Budget**.

Historical Preview of Indian Budget

- The term 'Budget' is actually derived from a French word *Bougette*, which means a sack or a pouch. It was first used in France in 1803.
- In the Constitution of India, the term 'Budget' is no where used. It is rather mentioned as Annual Financial Statement under comprising the Revenue Budget, Capital Budget and also the estimates for the next fiscal year called Budget Estimates.
- As per the British legacy, the Union Budget of India used to be presented on the evening of last working day of the month of February to follow the British Budget.
- The first Union Budget of independent India was presented by **RK Shanmukham Chetty** on 26th November, 1947.
- RK Shanmukham Chetty was served as the first Finance Minister of Independent India from 1947 to 1949.
- **Morarji Desai** has given budget for the maximum number of times (10 times).
- During the NDA regime, Finance Minister **Yashwant Sinha** was the first to present the budget on 28th February, 2001 at 11:00 AM.
- From the year 2017-18 and onwards, the Union Budget is presented by Union Finance Minister on 1st February of every year.
- The budget has to be passed by the Lok Sabha before it can come into effect on 1st April.
- The railway budget was merged with the general budget from the fiscal year 2017-18 based on the recommendation of the Bibek Debroy Committee.

Objectives of Government Budget

The following are the objectives of Government budgeting in India :

- **Reallocation of Resources** It helps to distribute resources keeping in view, the social and economic conditions of the country.
- **Reducing Inequalities in Income and Wealth** Government aims to bring economic equality by imposing taxes on the elite class and spending the collected money on the welfare of the poor.
- **Contributing to Economic Growth** A country's economic growth is based on the rate of investment and savings. Therefore, the budgetary plan focuses on preparing adequate resources for investing in the public sector and raising the overall rate of investments and savings.
- **Bringing Economic Stability** The Budget focuses on avoiding business fluctuations so as to accomplish the aim of financial stability. Policies such as Deficit Budget (during deflation) and Surplus Budget (during inflation) assist in balancing the prices in the economy.
- **Managing Public Enterprises** Many public sector industries are built for the social welfare of the people. The Budget is planned to deliver different provisions for operating such business and imparting financial help.
- **Reducing Regional Differences** It aims to reduce regional inequalities by promoting the installation of production units in the underdeveloped regions.

Types of Budget

Various types of budget are discussed below :

1. Traditional Budget

- A traditional budget indicates the amount of money you allot during a set time period for specific financial obligations, such as rent, entertainment or insurance.

- The budget is designed to help you spend your income according to a plan.
- A traditional budget starts with your income and lists the categories on which you expect to spend your money.
- At the end of the time period, it you keep accurate records, you should know how closely your spending matched your intentions.

2. Zero Based Budgeting

- It is a method of budgeting in which all expenses are evaluated each time a budget is made and expenses must be justified for each new period.
- Zero budgeting starts from the zero base and every function of the government is analysed for its needs and cost. Budget is then made based on the needs.

3. Outcome Budget

- It analyses the progress of each ministry and department and what the respected ministry has done with its Budget outlay.
- It measures the development outcomes of all government programmes.
- It was first introduced in the year 2005.

4. Performance Budgeting

- It is a method of budgeting that provides the purpose and objectives for which funds are needed i.e. costs of programmes and related activities proposed to accomplish those objectives and outputs to be produced or services to be rendered under each programme.

5. Gender-Budgeting

- It is defined as 'gender-based assessment of budgets, incorporating a gender perspective at all levels of the budgetary process and restructuring revenues and expenditures in order to promote gender equality'.
- It is actually budgeting for gender equity. Through Gender Budget, the government declares an amount to be spent over the development, welfare, empowerment schemes and programmes for females.

6. Balanced Budget

- A government budget is assumed to be balanced if the estimated expenditure is equal to the anticipated receipts for a fiscal year.

7. Surplus Budget

- A budget is said to be surplus when the expected revenues surpass the estimated expenditure for a particular business year.
- Here, the budget becomes surplus, when taxes imposed, are higher than the expenses.

8. Deficit Budget

- A Budget is in deficit if the expenditure surpasses the revenue for a designated year.

9. Sunset Budgeting

- In this type of budgeting, schemes are announced with deadline.
- They are terminated after approaching the prescribed time-frame.

Budget Formation in India

- A budget is a quantitative expression of a plan for a defined period of time. In India, it is done for one financial year from 1st April to 31st March.
- Finance Ministry starts preparing budget 5 to 6 months prior to financial year (September-October).
- Finance Ministry sends circular and forms to administrative affair and demand for its expenditure for the next financial year.
- Administrative affair sends these forms and circular to local and regional officer who fill the form about the expenditure and send it to the Finance Ministry.

Constitutional Fund in Budget

Constitutional fund in budget are as follows :

Consolidated Fund of India

- Consolidated Fund of India is the most important of all government accounts.
- Revenues received by the government and expenses made by it, excluding the exceptional items, are part of the Consolidated Fund.
- This fund was constituted under **Article 266 (1)** of the Constitution of India.
- All revenues received by the government by way of direct taxes and indirect taxes, money borrowed and receipts from loans given by the government flow into the Consolidated Fund of India.
- All government expenditure is made from this fund, except exceptional items which are met from the Contingency Fund or the Public Account.
- Importantly, no money can be withdrawn from this fund without the Parliament's approval.

Public Account of India

- Public Account of India accounts for flows for those transactions where the government is merely acting as a banker. This fund was constituted under **Article 266 (2)** of the Constitution.

- It accounts for flows for those transactions where the government is merely acting as a banker. Examples of those are provident funds, small savings and so on. These funds do not belong of the government.
- They have to be paid back at some time to their rightful owners.
- Due to this nature of the fund, expenditures from it are not required to be approved by Parliament.

Contingency Fund of India

- Contingency Fund is created as an impress account to meet some urgent or unforeseen expenditure of the government.
- This fund was constituted by the government under **Article 267** of the Constitution of India.
- This fund is at the disposal of the President. Any expenditure incurred from this fund requires a subsequent approval from the Parliament and the amount withdrawn is returned to the fund from the Consolidated Fund.

Components of Government Budget

Various components of government budget are classified under flow chart given below :

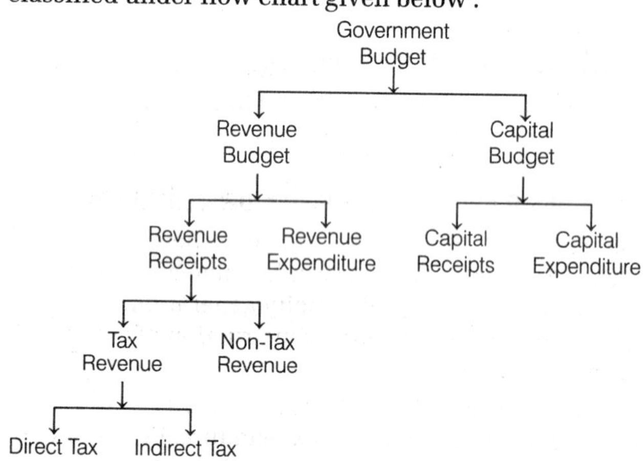

Revenue Budget

It consists of the **Revenue Receipts** and **Revenue Expenditure**.

Revenue Receipts

- These are receipts which do not have a direct impact on the assets and liabilities of the government.
- It consists of the money earned by the government through tax (such as excise duty and income tax) and non-tax sources (such as dividend income, profits and interest receipts).

Tax Revenue

- Tax is a compulsory payment that is made to the government by the people or the companies without having any direct benefit in return.
- The sum of all receipts from the taxes and all other duties under the government are referred to as tax revenue. They are either from direct taxes or indirect taxes.

Direct Taxes

- In India, direct taxes are levied on income and wealth.
- The most important direct tax from the point of view of revenue is personal **income tax** and **corporation tax**.
  - **Income Tax** Income tax is levied on the income of individuals, Hindu undivided families, unregistered firms and other associations of people. In India, the nature of income tax is progressive. For taxation purposes, income from all sources is added and taxed as per the income tax slabs of the individual.
  - **Corporation Tax** Corporation tax is levied on the income of corporate firms and corporations. For taxation purposes, A company is treated as a separate entity and thus must pay a separate tax different from the personal income tax of its owner. Companies both public and private which are registered in India under the Companies Act, 1956 are liable to pay corporate tax.

Indirect Taxes

- An indirect tax is a tax collected by an intermediary from the person who bears the ultimate economic burden of the tax. It can be shifted by the taxpayer to someone else.
- Some important indirect taxes imposed in India are as follows :
  - **Customs Duty** It is a tariff or tax imposed on goods when transported across international borders. The purpose of it is to protect the country's economy. Under the custom laws, the various types of duties are levied like Basic Duty, Countervailing Duty, Protective Duty, Anti-Dumping Duty, Export Duty.
  - **Central Excise Duty** It is the tax which is charged on excisable goods that are manufactured in India and are for domestic consumption.
  - **Service Tax** The Service Tax is levied on the gross amount charged by the service provider on the receiver.
  - **Sales Tax** Sales Tax in India is a form of tax that is imposed by the government on the sale or purchase of a particular commodity within the country. Sales Tax is imposed under both, Central and State Government Legislation.

- **Value Added Tax** (VAT) It is a tax on the estimated market value added to a product or material at each stage of its manufacture or distribution, ultimately which is passed on to the consumer.
- **Securities Transaction Tax** (STT) It is a tax levied on all transactions done on the stock exchanges.

Non-tax Revenue

- Non-tax revenue is the recurring income that is earned from sources other than taxes by the government.
- They are the revenue receipts that are not generated by taxing the public.
- Interests that are received by the government through the loans provided by it to the State Governments, Union Territories, private enterprises and the general public are an important source of non-tax revenue.
- Fees, fines, penalties, etc are also examples of non-tax revenue.

Tax on Wealth and Capital

- **Estate Duty** First introduced in 1953. It was levied on the total property passing on the death of a person. The whole property of the deceased person constitutes his wealth and is liable for the tax. The tax now stands abolished w.e.f 1985.
- **Wealth Tax** First introduced in 1957. It was levied on the excess of net wealth (over 30,00,00,0 @ 1%) of individuals, Joint Hindu families and companies. wealth tax has been a minor source of revenue. The tax now stands abolished w.e.f 2015.
- **Gift Tax** First introduced in 1958. The gift tax was levied on all donations except the one given by the charitable institution's government companies and private companies. The tax now stands abolished w.e.f 1998.
- **Capital Gain Tax** Any profit or gain that arises from the sale of the capital asset is a capital gain. The profit from the sale of capital is taxed. Capital asset includes land, building, house, jewellery, patents, copyrights, etc.
- **Short-term Capital Asset** An asset which is held for not more than 36 months or less is a short-term capital asset.
- **Long-term Capital Asset** An asset that is held for more than 36 months is a long-term capital asset.

Direct Taxes v/s Indirect Taxes

Basis	Direct Tax	Indirect Tax
Meaning	The tax that is levied by the government directly on the individuals or corporations are called direct taxes.	The tax that is levied by the government on one entity (Manufacturer of goods), but is passed on to the final consumer by the manufacturer.
Incidence	The incidence and impact of the direct tax fall on the same person.	The incidence and impact of the tax fall on different persons.
Examples	Income Tax, Corporation Tax and Wealth Tax.	VAT, Service tax, GST, Excise duty, entertainment tax and Customs Duty.
Nature	They are progressive in nature.	They are regressive in nature.
Objective	Both Social and Economical. Social objective of direct tax is the distribution of income. A person earning more should contribute more in the provision of public service by paying more tax. This provision is also known as progressive taxation.	Only Economical. When an indirect tax is levied on a product, both rich and poor must pay at the same rate. A person earning 10 lakh a month pays the same tax on the Wheat purchase as the person earning ₹ 3000 a month. This principle is called regressive taxation.
Impact	It is not at all inflationary.	It is inflationary.

Revenue Expenditure

It is the expenditure by the government which does not impact its assets or liabilities. For example, this includes salaries, interest payments, pension and administrative expenses.

Some Concepts Related to Expenditure

- **Plan Expenditure** All expenditures done in the name of planning (i.e., Five Year Plans) are called plan expenditures. For example, expenditure on electricity generation, irrigation and rural developments, construction of roads, bridges, canals, etc.
- **Non-Plan Expenditure** All expenditures other than plan expenditure are known as non-plan expenditure. For example, interest payments, pensions, statutory transfers to States Governments and Union Territories, etc.
- **Cess** Different from the usual taxes and duties like excise and personal income tax, a cess is imposed as an additional tax besides the existing tax (tax on tax) with a purpose of raising funds for a specific task. For example, the Swachh Bharat cess is levied by the government for cleanliness activities that it is undertaking across India.
- **Surcharge** The surcharge is a fee added to any tax that has already been paid. The surcharge is a term that refers to an extra fee or levy. A surcharge is a tax on tax that is not levied for any particular reason, and the proceeds of surcharges are used by the Union Government for whatever purpose it sees fit.

Goods and Services Tax (GST)

- The GST is a value-added tax levied on most goods and services sold for domestic consumption.
- The GST is paid by consumers, but it is remitted to the government by the businesses selling the goods and services. GST, which subsumed almost all domestic indirect taxes (e.g. petroleum, alcoholic beverages and stamp duty are the major exceptions) under one head, is perhaps the biggest tax reform in the history of independent India.
- It was launched into operation on the midnight of 1st July, 2017.

Types of GST

Under the GST form, four types of GST are

Central GST (CGST)

- Under the CGST, there is a provision to impose tax on the supply of goods and services by the Central Government.
- Earlier, Central Excise, Excise (Drugs and toilet construction), Excise duties on the taxes imposed by the Central Government, (Goods of special importance), additional duty of custom duty (known under CVD), Special Duty of Custom Duty (SAD), Service tax and gratuity surcharge related to the supply of goods or services. All these are now included in CGST.

State GST (SGST)

- Taxes imposed and collected by the State Government on goods and services are levied under State GST system.
- Earlier, State Governments used to levy VAT under State taxes, purchase tax, entry tax, entertainment tax, advertisement tax, including State excise and surcharge related to State sub-tax and imposition, lottery taxes, tax on speculation and gambling. All these taxes are now included in SGST.

Integrated GST (IGST, State Indemnification)

- The Goods and Services tax provides an integrated GST (IGST) levied on international commodities and services. It is imposed and recovered by the Central Government.
- The amount of taxes received under this is distributed to the State for the loss of revenue generated to the States.

Union Territory GST (UTGST)

- Arrangement or provision under the UTGST and Tax system is for the Union Territory where they do not have their own Legislative Assemblies, such as Andaman and Nicobar Island, Daman and Diu and Dadar and Nagar Haveli, etc.
- These Union Territories have the provision to levy and collect taxes by the Central Government.

Features of GST

Features of GST are as follows :

- **Applicable on Supply Side** GST is applicable on 'supply' of goods or services as against the old concept on the manufacture of goods or on sale of goods or on provision of services.
- **Destination based Taxation** GST is based on the principle of destination based consumption taxation as against the principle of origin-based taxation.
- **Dual GST** It is a dual GST with the centre and the states simultaneously levying tax on a common base. The GST to be levied by the Centre is called Central GST (CGST) and that to be levied by the States is called State GST (SGST).

  Import of goods or services would be treated as inter-state supplies and would be subject to Integrated Goods and Services Tax (IGST) in addition to the applicable customs duties.
- **GST rates to be mutually decided** CGST, SGST and IGST are levied at rates to be mutually agreed upon by the Central and the States. The rates are notified on the recommendation of the GST Council.
- **Multiple Rates** GST is levied at four rates i.e. 5%, 12%, 18% and 28%. The schedule or list of items that would fall under these multiple slabs are worked out by the GST Council. This is aside from the tax on gold that is kept at 3% and rough precious and semi-precious stones that are placed at a special rate of 0.25% under GST.

Taxes Replaced by GST

- The GST replaced the following Central taxes :
  - Central Excise Duty
  - Duties of Excise (Medicinal and Toilet Preparations)
  - Additional Duties of Excise (Goods of Special Importance)
  - Additional Duties of Excise (Textiles and Textile Products)
  - Additional Duties of Customs (commonly known as CVD)
  - Special Additional Duty of Customs (SAD)
  - Service Tax
  - Central Surcharges and Cesses so far as they relate to supply of goods and services
- State taxes subsumed under the GST are :
  - State VAT
  - Central Sales Tax
  - Luxury Tax
  - Entry Tax (all forms)

- Entertainment and Amusement Tax (except when levied by the local bodies)
- Taxes on advertisements e.g. Purchase Tax
- Taxes on lotteries, betting and gambling
- State Surcharges and Cesses so far as they relate to supply of goods and services

- Exemptions under GST :
  - Custom duty will still be collected along with the levy of IGST on imported goods.
  - Petroleum and tobacco products are currently exempted.
  - Excise duty on liquor, stamp duty and electricity taxes are also exempted.

Capital Budget

It includes the Capital Receipts and Capital Expenditure.

Capital Receipts

- It indicates the receipts which lead to a decrease in assets or an increase in liabilities of the government.
- It consists of :
  - the money earned by selling assets (or disinvestment) such as shares of public enterprises and
  - the money received in the form of borrowings or repayment of loans by States.

Capital Expenditure

- It is used to create assets or to reduce liabilities.
- It consists of :
  - the long-term investments by the government on creating assets such as roads and hospitals and
  - the money given by the government in the form of loans to States or repayment of its borrowings.

FRBM Act

- The Fiscal Responsibility and Budget Management Act, 2003 (FRBMA) is an act of the Parliament of India to institutionalise financial discipline, reduce India's fiscal deficit, improve macro-economic management and the overall management of the public funds by moving towards a balanced budget.
- Various **objectives related to FRBM Act** are as follows:
  - To reduce fiscal deficit and revenue deficit.
  - To achieve inter-generational equity in fiscal management by reducing the debt burden of the future generation.
  - To achieve long-term macro-economic stability.
  - Better co-ordination between fiscal and monetary policy.
  - Get transparency in fiscal operations of the government.

Amendments to FRBM Act

- Fiscal Responsibility and Budget Management Act, 2003 was amended in 2012.
- The amendment mandated the Central Government to lay the following before the Houses of Parliament :
  - Macro-Economic Framework Statement
  - Medium Term Fiscal Policy Statement
  - Fiscal Policy Strategy Statement along with the Annual Financial Statement
  - Demands for Grants
- The **NK Singh Committee**, which was set up in 2016 to review the FRBM Act, recommended that the government must target a fiscal deficit of 3% of the GDP in the years up to 31st March, 2020, subsequently cut it to 2.8% in 2020-21 and to 2.5% by 2023.

Recent Developments in Public Finance

Some of the important recent developments in Public Finance are as follows:

Interim Ways and Means Advances

- The Reserve Bank of India (RBI) has decided to continue with the existing interim Ways and Means Advances (WMA) scheme limit of ₹ 51,560 crore for all states/Union Territories upto September 2021, given the prevalence of COVID-19. The WMA scheme was introduced in 1997 to meet mismatches in the receipts and payments of the government.
- The government can avail immediate cash from the RBI, if required. But it has to return the amount within 90 days. Interest is charged at the existing repo rate.

GST Compensation

- The Centre distinguished the GST shortfall into two types:
  - Due to GST implementation itself.
  - Caused by the impact of COVID-19.
- The GST Compensation Act, 2017 guaranteed states that they would be compensated for any loss of revenue in the first five years of GST implementation, until 2022, using a cess levied on sin (harmful goods like tobacco, alcohol, cigarette, etc) and luxury goods.

Vivad se Vishwas Scheme

- The direct tax 'Vivad se Vishwas' Act, 2020 was enacted on 17th March, 2020, with the objective to reduce pending income tax litigation, generate timely revenue for the government and to benefit taxpayers.
- The scheme aims to end litigation and legacy disputes under the direct taxes category as ₹ 9.32 lakh crore worth of revenue is blocked in approximately 4.8 lakh appeals pending at various income tax appellate forums.

- The entities who opt for the scheme have to pay a requisite tax following which all litigation against them are closed by the tax department and penal proceedings dropped.

15th Finance Commission

- The government accepted the 15th Finance Commission's recommendation to maintain the States' share in the divisible pool of taxes to 41% for the five-year period starting 2021-22.
- The 15th Finance Commission was constituted by the President of India in November 2017, under the Chairmanship of NK Singh.
- Its recommendations will cover a period of five years from the year 2021-22 to 2025-26.
- It has recommended to maintaining the vertical devolution at 41%.

16th Finance Commission

- The Government of India According to Article 280 (1) of the Constitution of India, has established the 16th Finance Commission, appointing Dr. Arvind Panagariya as its chairperson.
- The commission has been requested to make its report available by 31st October, 2025.

Committees related to Fiscal Policy

Name of the Committees	Focus Areas
HR Khan Committee	Evaluates the unclaimed PPP and post office saving.
Justice MB Shah Commission	On black money.
Basel Committee	For banking supervision.
Dinesh Sharma Committee	Proposing new regulation related to virtual currencies or digital currencies.
Kelkar Committee	For tax structure reforms.
Nachiket Mor Committee	Providing financial services for low-income households and small businesses.
PJ Nayak Committee	Governance of boards in banks.
NK Singh Committee	To review the budget management act and fiscal responsibility.
Rattan P Watal Committee	Boosting the digital payment system in India.
SN Verma Committee (1999)	Restructuring the commercial banks.
Urjit Patel Committee	To examine the current monetary policy framework.
RH Khan Committee	For harmony among the roles of a financial institution in banks.
Raghuram Rajan Committee	For financial sector reforms.
SP Talwar Committee	For restructuring of weak public sector bank.

Extra Facts From Tamil Nadu Board and NIOS

- **Scope of Public Finance** : Public revenue, Public expenditure, Public debt, Financial administration and Fiscal policy.
- **Supplementary Budget** : During the time of war emergencies and natural calamities like tsunami, flood etc, the expenditures allotted in the budget provisions are not always enough. Under these circumstances, a supplementary budget can be presented by the Government to tackle these unforeseen events.
- **Vote - on - Account** : It is a special provision by which the Government gets permission from the Parliament to incur expenditures on necessary items till the budget is finally passed in the Parliament.
- **Process in the Preparation of the Budget** : Budget estimates are prepared by the Ministry of Finance>Based on the estimated income and expenditure of various ministries and departments, sent to the Ministry of Finance>Prepares Budget> Presented by the Finance Minister to the cabinet for approval>Budget is ready for presentation to the Parliament.
- The Public Accounts Committee and the Estimates Committee keep a constant vigil on the expenditure so that no Ministry or Department exceeds the amount sanctioned to it.
- According to Adam Smith, there are four canons or maxims of taxation. They are- Canons of Ability, Certainty, Convenience and Economy.
- **Merits of Direct Taxes** : Equity, Certainity, Elasticity and Economy.
- **Demerits of Direct Taxes** : Unpopular,Productivity affected, Inconvenient and Tax Evasion.
- **Merits of Indirect Taxes** : Wider Coverage, Equitable, Economical, Checks harmful consumption and Convenience.
- **Demerits of Indirect Taxes** : Higher cost of collection, Inelastic, Regressive, Uncertainity and No civic consciousness.
- **Finance Commission** : It a quasi-judicial body setup under Article 280 of the Indian Constitution. It was established in the year 1951, to define the fiscal relationship framework between the Central and the State.
  - It aims to reduce the fiscal imbalances between the Central and the States (Vertical imbalance) and also between the states (horizontal imbalance). It promotes inclusiveness.
  - A Finance Commission is set up once in every five years. It is normally constituted two years before the period. It is a temporary Body.

10

Foreign Trade and Balance of Payment

[SOURCES]

Class-IX & X Old NCERT Chap 4 (Towards Economic Development), Class-X New NCERT Chap 4 (Globalisation and the Indian Economy), Class-XI New NCERT Chap 1 (Indian Economy on the Eve of Independence), Chap 2 (Indian Economy 1950-1990), Class-XII New NCERT Chap 6 (Open Economy : Macroeconomics), Class-XII Old NCERT Chap 10 (Balance of Payment), Chap 9 (Foreign Exchange Rates : Meaning and Assessment) Tamil Nadu Board (Class-XII), NIOS

Foreign Trade

- Foreign trade or international trade is as old as human civilisation.
- Even in ancient times, when there were few means of transport, merchants from one country used to exchange goods with the other countries.
- Foreign trade is based on the theory of Comparative Costs.
- According to this theory, every country should try to produce goods which it can provide at a cost lower than other nations and should exchange supplies of such goods for goods which other countries can produce at a lower cost.
- Theory of Comparative Cost (Comparative Advantage) is regarded as the **Classical Theory of International Trade.**

Types of Foreign Trade

Foreign trade is divided into two types :

(i) **Visible trade** is trade in goods means, physical things that you can touch and weigh.

(ii) **Invisible trade** is trade in services like tourism and banking. Foreign trade has got an important place in the economic development of a country.

Components of Foreign Trade

Export and import are two important components of foreign trade.

Export

- It means a process whereby goods produced in one country are shipped to another country for sale or trade.
- Goods exported from India can be categorised into following four categories :
  - Agriculture and Allied product
  - Ore and Minerals
  - Manufactured Cotton and Silk Textiles and Handicraft
  - Fuel and Lubricants

Import

- It means a process by which goods services are brought from other country through purchase.
- Major items imported in India are as follows :
  - Petroleum and Allied Products
  - Edible oil and Fertiliser
  - Machine Tools, Electric and Non-Electric Machinery
  - Pearls, Precious and Semi-Precious Stones

Foreign Trade Policy (FTP)

- First time, Foreign Trade Policy was announced in 2004-05. Union Commerce Ministry, Government of India, announces integrated Foreign Trade Policy, also called **Export-Import** (EXIM) **Policy** every 5 year.

Foreign Trade Policy Formulation in India

- Foreign trade policy is formulated and implemented mainly by the Ministry of Commerce and Industry, alongwith other concerned Ministries and agencies, including the Ministry of Finance, the Ministry of Agriculture and the Reserve Bank of India.
- India considers FTP as an instrument to attain its overall economic policy objectives of growth, industrial development and self-sufficiency. However, India also uses FTP to attain short-term goals such as containing inflation.
- The mandate of the Department of Commerce, at the Ministry of Commerce and Industry, is to formulate India's International Trade and Commercial Policy and implement it.

New Foreign Trade Policy (2015-20)

- The Foreign Trade Policy, 2015-20 was announced by the Minister of Commerce and Industry, **Nirmala Sitharaman** on 1st April, 2015.
- The FTP has been announced in the backdrop of several measures initiated by the Government of India such as 'Make in India', 'Digital India' and 'Skills India', among others.
- The focus of the new policy is to support both the manufacturing and services sectors, with a special emphasis on improving the 'ease of doing business'.

Foreign Trade Policy (2021-26)

- The new Foreign Trade Policy 2021-26 came into effect from 1st April, 2021.
- The goal of the New Foreign Trade Policy is to make India a 5 trillion USD economy.
- Key highlights of the New Foreign Trade Policy are :
  - The District export hubs are to play a major role in the new Foreign Trade Policy.
  - The policy will aim to boost exports.
  - It will enhance ease of doing business.
  - It will bring improvements in the operations of the domestic manufacturing and services sector through infrastructure support.
  - The policy will bring changes to regulatory and operational framework and lower transaction costs.

India's Foreign Trade Position

- The goods trade deficit rose almost 40% to over US $ 266 billion in 2022-23, compared to US $ 190 billion in 2021-22.
- Total goods exports in 2022-23 was US $ 447.46 billion, while the import bill was US $ 714 billion.
- Petroleum products, electronic goods, rice, chemicals and drugs and pharmaceuticals were top export items from India.
- The USA remained India's top export destination followed by UAE and China.
- India's imports from Russia grew almost 370% to over US $ 46 billion in 2022-23. Its share of import increased from 1.6% in 2021-22 to 6.5% in 2022-23.
- The government has set a two trillion-dollars target for goods and services exports by 2030 under the new Foreign Trade Policy.

Top Export Destinations (Year 2022)

Country	Export %	Country	Export %
1. USA	18.05%	5. Netherlands	2.97%
2. UAE	6.65%	6. Singapore	2.64%
3. China	5.04%	7. Hong Kong	2.6%
4. Bangladesh	3.83%	8. United Kingdom	2.49%

Top Import Sources (Year 2022)

Country	Import %	Country	Import %
1. China	15.43%	5. Iraq	5.21%
2. UAE	7.31%	6. Switzerland	3.82%
3. USA	7.07%	7. Hong Kong	3.12%
4. Saudi Arabia	5.56%	8. Singapore	3.09%

Balance of Payment (BOP)

- The Balance of Payments (BOP) records the transactions in goods, services and assets between residents of a country with the rest of the world for a specified time period typically a year.
- It is the net outcome of the current and capital accounts of an economy. It might be favourable or unfavourable for the economy. However, negativity of the BoP does not mean it is unfavourable.
- A negative BOP is unfavourable for an economy if only the economy lacks the means to fill the gap of negativity.
- The BoP of an economy is calculated on the principles of accountancy (double-entry book-keeping) and looks like the balance sheet of a company—every entry shown either as credit (inflow) or debit (outflow).

- If there is a positive outcome at the end of the year, the money is automatically transferred to the foreign exchange reserves of the economy and if there is any negative outcome, the same foreign exchange is drawn from the country's forex reserves.

The Balance of Payment (BOP) Crisis of 1991 in India

- The Balance of Payment crisis occurs when there is insufficient capital account surplus and foreign exchange reserves for financing the current account deficit.
- India faced the BOP crisis in 1991 due to factors such as the Gulf War which increased the oil prices.
- The disintegration of the USSR also negatively impacted India's exports contributing to the BOP crisis.
- The value of the Indian rupee fell and the Reserve Bank of India sold its forex reserves for making the Balance of Payment zero. Since, the RBI did not have enough forex reserves, India had to pledge 65 tonnes of gold for getting foreign loans to make the Balance of Payment zero.

Components of BOP

Current account and capital account are the important components BOP.

Current Account

- Current Account is the record of trade in goods and services and transfer payments.
- Trade in goods includes exports and imports of goods.
- Trade in services includes factor income and non-factor income transactions.
- Transfer payments are the receipts which the residents of a country get for 'free', without having to provide any goods or services in return.
- They consist of gifts, remittances and grants. They could be given by the government or by private citizens living abroad.

Balance on Current Account

Balance on current account has following two components :

(i) **Balance of Trade** (BOT) **or Trade Balance** It is the difference between the value of exports and value of imports of goods of a country in a given period of time.
Export of goods is entered as a credit item in BoT, whereas import of goods is entered as a debit item in BoT.

(ii) **Balance on Invisibles** Net Invisibles is the difference between the value of exports and the value of imports of invisibles of a country in a given period of time. Invisibles include services, transfers and flows of income that take place between different countries.
Services trade includes both factor and non-factor income. Factor income includes net international earnings on factors of production (like labour, land and capital). Non-factor income is net sale of service products like shipping, banking, tourism, software services, etc.

Current Account Deficit (CAD)

- There is a deficit in Current Account if the value of the goods and services imported exceeds the value of those exported.
- It is measured as a percentage of GDP.
- The formula for calculating CAD is

Current Account Deficit = Trade Gap* + Net Current Transfers + Net Income Abroad

*Trade gap = Exports – Imports

- A country with rising CAD shows that it has become uncompetitive and investors may not be willing to invest there.
- In India, the Current Account Deficit could be reduced by boosting exports and curbing non-essential imports such as gold, mobiles and electronics.
- Current Account Deficit and Fiscal Deficit (also known as 'budget deficit' is a situation when a nation's expenditure exceeds its revenues) are together known as **twin deficits** and both often reinforce each other, i.e., A high fiscal deficit leads to higher CAD and *vice-versa*.

Capital Account

- Capital Account records all international transactions of assets. Purchase of assets is a debit item on the capital account. If an Indian buys a UK Car Company, it enters capital account transactions as a debit item (as foreign exchange is flowing out of India).
- On the other hand, the sale of assets like the sale of shares of an Indian company to a Chinese customer is a credit item on the capital account.

Components of Capital Account

The components of capital account are :

- **Borrowing and Lendings from Foreign Countries** It includes the financial transactions related to borrowing money from foreign countries by the private sector companies or individuals, government etc.
  - The receipts from abroad which include the repayment of loans from the foreign citizens etc., are shown as a credit in the capital account.

- The financial transactions dealing with lending to abroad by the private sector companies, individuals and the government and the repayment of loans taken from foreign countries is shown as a debit in the capital account.

- **Investments to and from the Foreign Countries** The investments from the foreign countries in the Indian companies, government bonds, real estate, etc., in India are shown as a credit in the capital account as they lead to the inflow of foreign exchange.
  - The investments made by the Indian residents in the stocks and shares of companies abroad, government bonds, real estate etc. are shown as a debit in the capital account as they lead to the outflow of foreign exchange.
- **Foreign Direct Investment** (FDI) When the foreign residents buy Indian capital assets such as companies, industrial complexes, machines etc., it is shown as a credit to the capital account.
  - The FDI investment made by Indians in the foreign countries is shown as a debit in the capital account.
- **Foreign Portfolio Investment** (FPI) When the foreign residents purchase stocks, government bonds, corporate securities etc., then these transactions are shown as a credit to the capital account.
  - When Indian residents purchase securities and bonds in foreign countries, it is shown as a debit in the capital account.
- **Participatory Notes or P-Notes** These are financial instruments used by investors or hedge funds, that are not registered with the Securities and Exchange Board of India (SEBI) to invest in Indian securities.
  - India-based brokerages buy India-based securities and then issue participatory notes to foreign investors.
- **Changes in the Foreign Exchange Reserves** The foreign exchange reserves are the financial assets held by the Central Bank (RBI for India) of the country.
  - These reserves serve as financing items in the Balance of Payments.
  - Any withdrawal from the foreign exchange reserves is shown as credit, while any addition in the reserves is shown as a debit in the capital account.
  - The changes in foreign exchange reserves are shown in the BoP account and not the actual foreign exchange reserves.

Difference between Foreign Direct Investment and Foreign Portfolio Investment

Foreign Portfolio Investment	Foreign Direct Investment
Foreign Portfolio Investment or FPI refers to the investment made in the financial assets of an enterprise, based in one country, by the foreign investors.	Foreign Direct Investment or FDI pertains to international investment in which the investor obtains a lasting interest in an enterprise in another country.
An investor is inactive.	An investor is active.
Indirect investments in assets are made.	Direct investments in assets are made.
Investments made are short term in nature.	Investments made are long-term in nature.
It is volatile in nature.	It is stable in nature.

Balance on Capital Account

- Capital account is in balance when capital inflows (like receipt of loans from abroad, sale of assets or shares in foreign companies) are equal to capital outflows (like repayment of loans, purchase of assets or shares in foreign countries).
- Surplus in capital accounts arises when capital inflows are greater than capital outflows, whereas deficit in capital account arises when capital inflows are lesser than capital outflows.

Other Concepts related to Balance of Payments

- **Official Reserve Sale** The country could use its reserves of foreign exchange in order to balance any deficit in its Balance of Payments. The Reserve Bank sells foreign exchange when there is a deficit. This is called the Official Reserve Sale.
- **Autonomous Transaction** International economic transactions are called autonomous when transactions are made due to some reason other than to bridge the gap in the Balance of Payments, that is, when they are independent of the state of BoP.
- **Accommodating Transactions** These are determined by the gap in the Balance of Payments, that is, whether there is a deficit or surplus in the Balance of Payments.
- **Errors and Omissions** It is difficult to record all international transactions accurately. Thus, we have a third element of BoP (apart from the current and capital accounts) called errors and omissions which reflects this.

Present Status of Balance of Payments in India

- The reforms of 1990's have facilitated India to move away from closed economy framework towards a more open and liberal economy.
- Foreign exchange reserves were built to very comfortable positions and the difficulties of BoP came under control.

- The important reasons for deficit in India's BoP position can be cited as follows:
  - **Irreversible Trade Deficit** Our imperative imports of oil and coal and India's passion for gold.
  - **Rise in Imports** The reasons for rapid rise in imports are building industrial base (in the early stages), increase in export related imports (gems, jewellery, capital goods) increase in imports of industrial raw materials, rise in the price and imports of Petroleum, Oil and Lubricants (POL) products etc.
  - **Devaluation and Depreciation of the Rupee** The devaluation and depreciation of the rupee have led to an increase in the price of imports. Exports have become cheaper, the low price and income elasticities of demand for exports have resulted in slow increase in exports.
  - **Slow Rise in Export Earnings** Export earnings rose, however, they were not sufficient enough to meet the rising imports. Thus, rise in exports has neither been substantial nor continuous. The growth in exports has not been sufficient enough to finance the rising imports.
  - **Debt Service** The Balance of Payments (BoP) problem has also aggravated due to the rising obligation of amortising payments in 2011-12, debt service ratio was 6% with the ever increasing imports and slow pace of exports, the most effective solution for India's Balance of Payments (BoP) problem is cost reduction and competitiveness in global market.
  - **Appreciation** The recent appreciation of the rupee has made exports costlier and imports cheaper. It may also add to the Balance of Payments (BoP) problem.

Currency Convertibility

- Currency convertibility is the ease with which the currency of a country can be freely converted into any other foreign currency or gold, at market determined exchange rate based on demand and supply for that currency.
- Convertibility of Indian rupee is the ease with which rupee can be converted into any foreign exchange like US dollars, Pound Sterling, Euro, etc and *vice-versa*.

Current Account Convertibility

- It refers to the freedom in payments and transfers in the current account international transactions.
- At present, current account is completely convertible (operationalised on 19th August, 1994).
- It means that the full amount of the foreign exchange required by someone for current purposes will be made available to him at the official exchange rate and there could be an unprohibited outflow of foreign exchange (earlier it was partially convertible).
- India was obliged to do so as per Article 8 of the International Monetary Fund (IMF) which prohibits any exchange restrictions on current international transactions (keep in mind that India was under pre-conditions of the IMF since 1991).
- Some restrictions from the **Foreign Exchange Management Act** (FEMA), 1999 are still applicable. These restrictions include non-convertibility for activities such as betting, gambling and on prohibited items. Different limits have been imposed on convertibility in the current account for travelling to other countries, sending gifts, educational purposes, employment and medical treatment etc.

Capital Account Convertibility

- It is the freedom to convert the local financial assets into foreign financial assets at the market determined exchange rates. Full capital account convertibility would ultimately lead to unrestricted movement of capital.
- After the recommendations of the **SS Tarapore Committee** (1997) on Capital Account Convertibility, India has been moving in the direction of allowing full convertibility in this account, but with required precautions.
- Conditions to be fulfilled before adopting full Capital Account Convertibility in India are as follows :
  - The government should reduce the fiscal deficit to 3.5% of the GDP. The committee recommended setting up the Consolidated Sinking Fund (CSF) for the reduction of government debt.
  - It recommended mandated inflation targeting between 3% to 5%. The RBI was to be given full freedom for using monetary policy tools for achieving this inflation target.
  - The committee recommended strengthening the financial sector by deregulating the interest rates, reducing the Non-Performing Assets to 5 and the Cash Reserve Ratio to 3%. It recommended either the liquidation of weak banks or their merger with other strong banks.
  - The Current Account Deficit should be brought down to manageable limits and the debt service ratio to be reduced to 20 % from the present 25% of the export earnings.

FERA and FEMA Act

- FERA (Foreign Exchange Regulation Act), 1974 was not successful in restricting activities such as the expansion of Trans National Corporations (TNCs).
- After the Amendment of FERA in 1993, it was decided that the act would become the FEMA (Foreign Exchange Management Act).

- This was done in order to relax the controls on foreign exchange in India, as a result of economic liberalisation. FEMA served to make transactions for external trade (exports and imports) easier. Involving current account for external trade no longer required RBI's permission.
- The deals in foreign exchange were to be 'managed' instead of 'regulated'.
- The switch to FEMA shows the change on the part of the government in terms of foreign capital.
- The foreign Exchange Regulation Act (FERA) was a legislation passed by the Indian Parliament in 1973 and come into force on 1st January, 1974.
- FERA imposed strict regulation on certain kinds of payments.
- It deals with foreign exchange and scousitles and the transactions which had an impact on the foreign exchange and import and export of currency.
- The Foreign Exchange Management Act (FEMA) was an act passed in the winter session of parliament in 1999 which replaced foreign exchange Regulation Act.
- FEMA has brought a new management regime of foreign exchange consistent with the emerging frame work of the World Trade Organisation (WTO).

Foreign Exchange Market

- The market in which national currencies are traded for one another is known as the foreign exchange market.
- The major participants in the foreign exchange market are commercial banks, foreign exchange brokers and other authorised dealers and monetary authorities.

Foreign Exchange Rate

- Foreign Exchange Rate (also called Forex Rate) is the price of one currency in terms of another.
- It links the currencies of different countries and enables comparison of international costs and prices. *For example*, if we have to pay ₹ 50 for $1 then the exchange rate is ₹ 50 per dollar.
- A rise in the price of foreign exchange will increase the cost (in terms of rupees) of purchasing a foreign good.
- This reduces demand for imports and hence demand for foreign exchange also decreases, other things remaining constant.
- A rise in the price of foreign exchange will reduce the foreigner's cost (in terms of USD) while purchasing products from India, other things remaining constant.
- This increases India's exports and hence supply for foreign exchange may increase.

Determination of the Exchange Rate

Different countries have different methods of determining their currency's exchange rate. It can be determined through Flexible Exchange Rate, Fixed Exchange Rate or Managed Floating Exchange Rate.

Fixed Exchange Rate

- Under the fixed exchange rate regime, the government or the Central bank has complete intervention in the determination of the currency's exchange rate.
- This is achieved by linking the domestic currency to the value of gold or with other major currencies such as the US dollar etc.
- The government has the responsibility to intervene and maintain the exchange rate equilibrium in case of any fluctuations due to any reason. The benefit of the fixed exchange rate regime is that it ensures stability in the exchange rate of the domestic currency.
- It ensures that the domestic currency does not appreciate or depreciate beyond the predetermined level. Fixed exchange rate regime has the disadvantage that it puts a massive burden on the government for maintenance of the exchange rate and the government may have to infuse a large amount of money for the maintenance of the exchange rates.
- The foreign investment can reduce under the fixed exchange rate regime as investors may lose their confidence if they believe that the exchange rate of the domestic currency does not represent the real value of the economy.

Floating Exchange Rate

- Under the floating exchange rate regime, the market forces determine the value of domestic currency on the basis of the forces of demand and supply of the domestic currency.
- In this system, neither the government nor the central bank intervenes and the market functions freely determine the real value of domestic currency.
- The floating exchange rate regime establishes trust among the foreign investors which can help in the increase in foreign investment in the domestic economy.
- This system ensures that a country can get easy access to loans from the IMF and other international financial institutions.

Managed Floating Exchange Rate

- Managed floating exchange rate regime lies between the fixed exchange rate regime and the floating exchange rate regime.
- In this system, the exchange rate of domestic currency is allowed to move freely based on the market forces of demand and supply.

- However, during difficult circumstances, the Central Bank intervene to stabilise the exchange rate of the domestic currency.
- It can further be categorised as follows :
  - **Adjusted Peg System** Under this, the Central Bank tries to hold the exchange rate of domestic currency until the foreign exchange reserves of that country gets exhausted. After this, the Central Bank goes for the devaluation of the domestic currency to move to another equilibrium of the exchange rate.
  - **Crawling Peg System** Under this, the Central Bank keeps on adjusting exchange rate based on the new demand and supply conditions of the exchange rate market. It follows a system of regular checks and balances and the Central Bank undertakes small devaluations based on the market conditions.
  - **Clean Floating** Under this, the exchange rate of domestic currency is based on the market forces of demand and supply without the government intervention. This system is identical to the floating exchange rate.
  - **Dirty Floating** Under this, the exchange rate is mainly determined by the market forces of demand and supply but the Central Bank occasionally intervened to remove excessive fluctuations from the foreign exchange markets.

Exchange Rate Management in India

The exchange rate management system in India has undergone a systematic change since Independence from the system of the pegged exchange rate to the present form of market determined exchange rate after liberalisation in 1993. These changes are :

- **Par Value System Till 1971** Under this system, the external value of rupee was fixed by the government to the UK pound sterling and gold. In 1966, the Indian Rupee was devalued by 36 %.
- **Pegged Regime** (1971-1992) The value of Indian rupee was pegged to US dollar (1971-1991) and to the pound sterling (1971-1975). After the breakdown of the Bretton Woods System and the collapse of the pound sterling, the value of Indian rupee was pegged on the basis of the weighted average of a basket of currencies of the major trading partners of India. The RBI determined the exchange rate within a band of plus minus 5 % of this weighted average.
- **Partial Convertibility After 1991** Partial convertibility of Indian rupee was in operation till 1993 under the Liberalised Exchange Rate Management System (LERMS). In this system, 40 % of the exchange rate was to be converted on the basis of the official exchange rate and the remaining 60 % was based on the market determined exchange rate.
- **Market Based Exchange Rate Regime Since 1993** India adopted the market based exchange rate in 1993 and the LERMS was removed in the budget 1994. RBI intervenes in the market only to reduce volatility and sudden appreciation or depreciation of Indian rupee.

Other Concepts Related to Exchange Rate

The other concepts related to exchange rate are :

- **Nominal Effective Exchange Rate** (NEER) **and Real Effective Exchange Rate** (REER) The indices NEER and REER are used as indicators of external competitiveness.
  - NEER is the weighted average of bilateral nominal exchange rates of the home currency in terms of foreign currencies.
  - The REER, defined as a weighted average of nominal exchange rates adjusted for relative price differential between the domestic and foreign countries, relates to the Purchasing Power Parity (PPP) hypothesis.
  - These are prepared jointly in the Division of International Finance, Department of Economic Analysis and Policy and the Department of External Investments and Operations, Reserve Bank of India.
- **The Gold Standard** From around 1870 to the outbreak of the First World War in 1914, the prevailing system was the gold standard which was the epitome of the fixed exchange rate system.
  - All currencies were defined in terms of gold.
  - Each participant country committed to guarantee the free convertibility of its currency into gold at a fixed price.
- **Special Drawing Rights** (SDRs) The SDR is an international reserve asset, created by the IMF in 1969 to supplement its member countries' official reserves.
  - The value of the SDR is based on a basket of five currencies i.e. the US dollar, the Euro, the Chinese renminbi, the Japanese yen and the British pound sterling.

Mayaram Committee Report on Foreign Trade

- This report on foreign trade was accepted by Government of India in 2014. According to it, foreign investment of 10% or more in a listed company will now be treated as FDI.
- An investor may be allowed to invest below 10% and this can be treated as FDI subject to the condition that the FDI stake is raised to 10% or beyond within one year from the date of the first purchase.
- If the stake is not raised to 10% or above, then the investment can be treated as portfolio investment.
- Foreign Portfolio Investors include Foreign Institutional Investors (FIIs) and Qualified Foreign Investors (QFIs).
- Foreign investment in an unlisted company, irrespective of the threshold limit, may be treated as FDI.

Extra Facts From Tamil Nadu Board and NIOS

Trade Blocks

- **Free Trade Area** It is the region encompassing a trade block whose member countries have signed a Free-Trade Agreement (FTA). Such agreements involve cooperation between atleast two countries to reduce trade barriers. E.g., SAFTA, EFTA.
- **Customs Union** It is defined as a type of trade block which is composed of a free trade area with no tariff among members and (zero tariffs among members) with a common external tariff. E.g., BENELUX (Belgium, Netherland and Luxembourg).
- **Common Market** It is established through trade pacts. A group formed by countries within a geographical area to promote duty free trade and free movement of labour and capital among its members. E.g., European Common Market (ECM).
- **Economic Union** It is composed of a common market with a customs union. The participant countries have both common policies on product regulation, freedom of movement of goods, services and the factors of production and a common external trade policy. (E.g., European Economic Union)

Balance of Payment (BOP) Disequilibrium

- When receipts are less than payments, the BOP is said to be unfavourable or adverse. That is called balance of payments disequilibrium.
- Types of BOP Disequilibrium
  - **Cyclical Disequilibrium** Cyclical disequilibrium occurs because of two reasons.
    First, two countries may be passing through different phases of the business cycle. Secondly, the elasticities of demand may differ between countries.
  - **Secular Disequilibrium** The secular or long-run disequilibrium in BOP occurs because of long-run and deep seated changes in an economy as it advances from one stage of growth to another. In the initial stages of development, domestic investment exceeds domestic savings and imports exceed exports, as it happens in India since 1951.
  - **Structural Disequilibrium** Structural changes in the economy may also cause balance of payments disequilibrium. Such structural changes include the development of alternative sources of supply, the development of better substitutes, the exhaustion of productive resources or changes in transport routes and costs.

Correction of Disequilibrium in BOP

- **Automatic Correction** Price adjustments, interest rate adjustments, income adjustments and capital flows.
- **Deliberate Measures**
  - **Monetary Measures** Monetary contraction / expansion, devaluation/ revaluation and exchange control.
  - **Miscellaneous Measures** Foreign loans, incentives for foreign investment, tourism development, incentives for foreign remittances, import substitution.
- **Trade Measures**
  - **Export Promotion** Abolition /reduction of duties, export subsidies, export incentives.
  - **Import Control** Import duties, import quotas, import prohibition.
- **FOREX** It is the system or process of converting one national currency into another, and of transferring money from one country to another.
- **Determinants of Exchange Rate**
  (1) Differentials in inflation
  (2) Differential in interest rates
  (3) Current account deficits
  (4) Public debt
  (5) Terms of trade
  (6) Political and economic stability
  (7) Recession
  (8) Speculation.
- **Foreign Institutional Investment (FII)** It is an investment in hedge funds, insurance companies, pension funds and mutual funds. Foreign institutional investment is a common term in the financial sector of India.
  For example, a mutual fund in the United States can invest in an India-based company.

11

Liberalisation, Privatisation and Globalisation

(SOURCES)

Class-X New NCERT Chap 4 (Globalisation and the Indian Economy), Class-XI New NCERT Chap 3 (Liberalisation, Privatisation and Globalisation : An Appraisal) Tamil Nadu Board (Class-XI), NIOS

Economic Reforms, 1991

- The economic reforms which changed the path of the economy that the country witnessed in later years were the LPG reforms.
- The LPG (Liberalisation, Privatisation, Globalisation) sometimes also referred to as LPGM where, M stands for Marketisation introduced in 1991 during the crisis that affected the government.

Factors Responsible for Economic Reforms

Factors responsible for economic reforms are

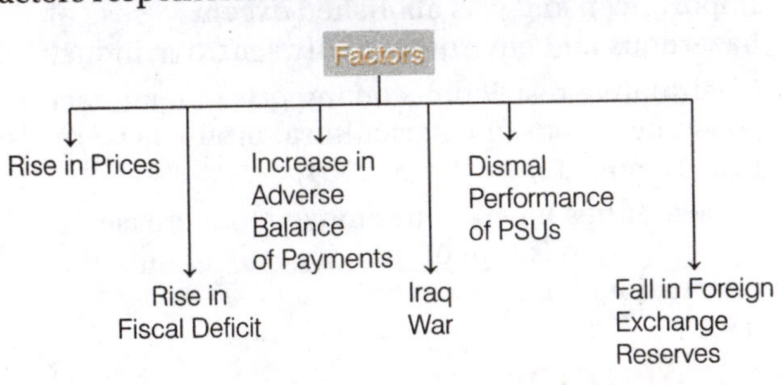

- **Rise in Prices** The inflation rate increased from 6.7% to 16.7% during 1980s and the country's economic position became worse.
- **Rise in Fiscal Deficit** Due to increase in non-development expenditure, the fiscal deficit of the government increased. Due to the rise in fiscal deficit, there was a rise in public debt and interest. In 1991, interest liability became 36.4% of total government expenditure.
- **Increase in Adverse Balance of Payments** In 1980-81, it was ₹ 2,214 crores and rose in 1990- 91 to ₹ 17,367 crores.
- To cover this deficit a large amount of foreign loans had to be obtained and the interest payment got increased.
- **Iraq War** In 1990-91, war in Iraq broke, which led to a rose in petrol prices. The flow of foreign currency from Gulf countries stopped and this further aggravated the problem.
- **Dismal Performance of PSUs** These were not performing well due to political interference and became a big liability for the government.
- **Fall in Foreign Exchange Reserves** India's foreign exchange reserve fell to low level in 1990-91 and it was insufficient to pay for an import bill for 2 weeks.

Liberalisation

- Economic liberalisation refers to a situation where unnecessary restrictions and controls are removed from a country's economy to ensure that businesses and enterprises can maximise their contribution. However, it is important to note that liberalisation does not mean an uncontrolled economy.
- The Indian economy was liberalised in the year 1991. In India, the concept of economic liberalisation was introduced to attain several objectives i.e., industrialisation, expansion in the role of private and foreign investment and introducing a free market system.

- Restrictions were relaxed for private companies to enter several core industries, which were previously reserved for the public sector.

Objectives of Liberalisation in India

The primary objectives of initiating liberalisation in India can be summarised as follows

- To solve India's impending Balance of Payment (BoP) crisis and boost the private sector's participation in the development of India's economy.
- To increase the volume of Foreign Direct Investment (FDI) in India's businesses and introduce competition between India's domestic businesses.
- To maximise India's economic potential by encouraging multinational and private companies to expand.
- To usher in globalisation for the Indian economy and regulate export and import and promote foreign trade.

Liberalisation Measures in India

Though a few liberalisation measures were introduced in the 1980s in areas of industrial licensing, export-import policy and foreign investment, reform policies initiated in 1991 were more comprehensive. These measures are :

De-regulation of Industrial Sector

- Industrial licensing was abolished for almost all except product categories alcohol, cigarettes, hazardous chemicals, industrial explosives, electronics, aerospace and drugs and pharmaceuticals.
- The only industries which are now reserved for the public sector are a part of atomic energy generation and some core activities in railway transport.
- Many goods produced by small-scale industries have now been dereserved.
- In most industries, the market has been allowed to determine the prices.

Financial Sector Reforms

- The reform policies led to the establishment of private sector banks, Indian as well as foreign. Foreign investment limit in banks was raised to around 74%.
- Those banks which fulfil certain conditions have been given freedom to set up new branches without the approval of the RBI and rationalise their existing branch networks.
- Though banks have been given permission to generate resources from India and abroad, certain managerial aspects have been retained with the RBI to safeguard the interests of the account-holders and the nation.
- Foreign Institutional Investors (FII), such as merchant bankers, mutual funds and pension funds, are now allowed to invest in Indian financial markets.

Tax Reforms

- The rate of corporation tax, which was very high earlier, has been gradually reduced.
- Efforts have also been made to reform the indirect taxes, taxes levied on commodities, in order to facilitate the establishment of a common national market for goods and commodities.
- In 2016, the Indian Parliament passed a law, Goods and Services Tax (GST) Act, 2016 to simplify and introduce a Unified Indirect Tax System in India.
- This is expected to generate additional revenue for the government, reduce tax evasion and create 'one nation, one tax and one market'.
- In order to encourage better compliance on the part of taxpayers, many procedures have been simplified and the rates were also lowered substantially.

Foreign Exchange Reforms

- In 1991, as an immediate measure to resolve the Balance of Payments crisis, the rupee was devalued against foreign currencies.
- This led to an increase in the inflow of foreign exchange.
- It also set the tone to free the determination of rupee value in the foreign exchange market from government control.

Trade and Investment Policy Reforms

- The trade policy reforms aimed at :
  - dismantling of quantitative restrictions on imports and exports,
  - reduction of tariff rates and,
  - removal of licensing procedures for imports.
- Import licensing was abolished except in case of hazardous and environmentally sensitive industries.
- Quantitative restrictions on imports of manufactured consumer goods and agricultural products were also fully removed from April, 2001.
- Export duties have been removed to increase the competitive position of Indian goods in the international markets.

Privatisation

- It implies shedding of the ownership or management of a government owned enterprise by private companies.
- Various features of privatisation are as follows :
  - Government companies are converted into private companies in two ways :
    (a) By withdrawal of the government from ownership and management of public sector companies.

(b) By outright sale of public sector companies.

- Privatisation of the public sector enterprises by selling off part of the equity of PSEs to the public is known as disinvestment.
- The government has also made attempts to improve the efficiency of PSUs by giving them autonomy in taking managerial decisions. For instance, some PSUs have been granted special status as maharatnas, navratnas and miniratnas.

- The following are the objectives of privatisation :
  - To reduce the financial burden on the government.
  - To improve public finances.
  - To introduce competition and market discipline.
  - To de-politicise non-essential services.
  - To encourage a wider share of ownership.

Privatisation and Disinvestment

- **Privatisation** implies a change in ownership, resulting in a change in management. The privatisation of public sector enterprises will occur only when the government sells more than 51% of its ownership to private entrepreneurs.
- **Disinvestment**, on the other hand, has a much wider connotation as it could either involve dilution of the government stake to a level that results in a transfer of management or could also be limited to such a level as would permit government to retain control over the organisation.
- Disinvestment beyond 50% involves the transfer of management, whereas disinvestment below 50% would result in the government continuing to have a major say in the undertaking.
- Minority and majority are the two types of disinvestment i.e.,
  - **Minority Disinvestment** A minority disinvestment is one such that, at the end of it, the government retains a majority stake in the company, typically greater than 51%, thus ensuring management control.
  - **Majority Disinvestment** A majority disinvestment is one in which the government, post disinvestment, retains a minority stake in the company i.e., it sells off a majority stake.

Globalisation

- Although, globalisation is generally understood to mean integration of the economy of the country with the world economy, it is a complex phenomenon.
- It is an outcome of the set of various policies that are aimed at transforming the world towards greater interdependence and integration.
- It involves creation of networks and activities transcending economic, social and geographical boundaries.

Effects of Globalisation in India

- Owing to globalisation, many Indian companies have expanded their wings to many other countries. For example, ONGC Videsh, a subsidiary of the Indian public sector enterprise, Oil and Natural Gas Corporation engaged in Oil and Gas exploration and production has projects in 16 countries.
- The low wage rates and availability of skilled manpower in India have made it a destination for global outsourcing in the post-reform period.
- Increase in flow of investments from developed countries to India is used for economic reconstruction.
- Technological development has resulted in reverse brain-drain in India.

Disadvantages of Globalisation

- Due to globalisation, the number of rural landless families increased from 35% in 1987 to 45 % in 1999, further to 55% in 2005.
- The farmers are destined to die of starvation or suicide.

New Strategic Disinvestment Policy, 2021

- This Policy aims to maintain 'bare minimum' presence in strategic sectors like atomic energy, defence, etc
- It also aims to exit from non-strategic sector and enterprises.

Outcomes of LPG Reforms

Some important positive and negative outcomes of the LPG reforms in India are as follows :

Positive Outcomes

- India's GDP growth rate increased. During 1990-91, India's GDP growth rate was only 1.1% but after 1991 reforms, GDP growth rate increased year by year and in 2015-16, it was estimated to be 7.5% by the IMF.
- Since 1991, India has firmly established itself as a lucrative foreign investment destination. India gets the highest annual FDI inflows of US $ 83.57 billion in FY 21-22. During FY 2022-23 FDI inflow of $ 71 billion has been reported.
- In 1991, the unemployment rate was high but after India adopted a new LPG policy, more employment got generated as new Foreign Companies came to India and due to liberalisation, many new entrepreneurs started companies.
- Per capita income increased due to an increase in employment. India's overall exports (merchandise and services combined) was 776.3 billion in FY 2022-23 which is the highest in term of overall export until now.

Negative Outcomes

- Since 1991, share of agriculture in the GDP has gone down drastically to 18%.
- This has resulted in lowering the per capita income of the farmers and increasing the rural indebtedness.
- Due to opening up of the Indian economy to foreign competition, more MNCs are competing with local businesses and companies which are facing problems due to financial constraints, lack of advanced technology and production line.
- Globalisation has also contributed to the destruction of the environment through pollution by emissions from manufacturing plants and clearing of vegetation cover.
- LPG policies have led to widening income gaps within the country.
- The higher growth rate is achieved by an economy at the expense of declining incomes of people who may be rendered redundant.

Extra Facts From Tamil Nadu Board and NIOS

Impact of LPG on Agricultural Sector Reforms

- Since the inception of economic reforms, the Indian economy has achieved a remarkable rate of growth in industry and service sector. However, this growth process bypassed the agricultural sector, which showed a sharp deceleration in the growth rate.
- The sector has recorded wide variations in yield and productivity and there was a shift towards cash crop cultivation.
- The agricultural indebtedness pushed several farming households into poverty and some of them resorted to extreme measures like suicides. Other agrarian crisis after reforms: High input costs, cutback in agricultural subsidies, reduction of import duties and paucity of credit facilities.

Fiscal Reforms After LPG

- It introduced fiscal discipline and aimed at reduction of fiscal deficit.
- The budget aimed at containing government expenditure and augmenting revenues; reversing the downtrend in the share of direct taxes to total tax revenues and curbing conspicuous consumption.
- Some of the important policy initiatives introduced for correcting the fiscal imbalance were: reduction in fertiliser subsidy, abolition of subsidy on sugar and disinvestment of a part of the government's equity holdings in select public sector undertakings.
- Gradually expenditures on welfare measures were reduced, tasks on corporate sectors were reduced and tasks on poor people were increased.

Monetary and Financial Sector Reforms After LPG

- Monetary reforms aimed at doing away with interest rate distortions and rationalising the structure of lending rates.
- New accounting norms regarding the classification of assets and provisions of bad debt were introduced in tune with the Narasimham Committee Report.
- Reduction in Statutory Liquidity Ratio (SLR) and the Cash Reserve Ratio (CRR) were recommended by the Narasimham Committee Report, 1991.

12

International Organisations

[SOURCES]

Class-X New NCERT Chap 4 (Globalisation and the Indian Economy), Class XI New NCERT Chap 3 (Liberalisation, Privatisation and Globalisation : An Appraisal), Class XI New NCERT Chap 8 (Comparative Development Experiences of Indian and Its Neighbours)
Tamil Nadu Board (Class-XII), NIOS

Introduction

- An international economic organisation is a forum of cooperation of sovereign states based on multilateral international agreement and comprises relatively stable range of participants.
- The organisations such as the IMF, the World Bank and other multilateral development banks; are heavily involved in 'managing' financial crises.
- These organisations try to assess national economies in, order to prevent fundamental issues that can affect the growth and stability of the world economy.

World Bank Group

- The World Bank Group (WBG) is a family of five international organisations that provide loans to developing countries.
- It is the largest and most famous development bank in the world and is an observer at the United Nations Development Group.
- Its five organisations are the International Bank for Reconstruction and Development (IBRD), the International Development Association (IDA), the International Finance Corporation (IFC), the Multilateral Investment Guarantee Agency (MIGA) and the International Centre for Settlement of Investment Disputes (ICSID).

International Bank for Reconstruction and Development (IBRD)

- IBRD provides loans and other assistance primarily to middle income and credit-worthy poor countries.
- Its interest rates are slightly lower than that offered by other financial institutions but with long-term maturity.
- IBRD was created in 1944 to help Europe reconstruct/rebuild after World War II. To be a member of IBRD, a country has to first join the International Monetary Fund (IMF).

Various functions of IBRD are as follows :

- It works closely with the rest of the World Bank Group to help developing countries reduce poverty, promote economic growth and build prosperity.
- It supports long-term human and social development that private creditors do not finance.
- It preserves borrowers' financial strength by providing support in times of crisis, when poor people are most adversely affected.
- It promotes policy and institutional reforms (such as safety net or anti-corruption reforms).
- It creates a favourable investment climate to catalyse the provision of private capital.
- It facilitates access to financial markets often at more favourable terms than members can achieve on their own. Its resources of the Bank consist of the capital and borrowings.

International Development Association (IDA)

- The International Development Association (IDA) is the part of the World Bank group that helps the under-developed and developing countries in the world.
- Overseen by 174 shareholder nations, IDA aims to reduce poverty by providing loans (credits) and grants for programmes that boost economic growth, reduce inequalities and improve people's living conditions.
- IDA complements the World Bank's original lending arm—the International Bank for Reconstruction and Development (IBRD).
- IBRD and IDA share the same staff and headquarters and evaluate projects with the same rigorous standards.
- IDA is one of the largest sources of assistance for the world's poorest countries, 39 of which are in Africa and is the single largest source of donor funds for basic social services in these countries.
- IDA lends money on concessional terms. This means that IDA credits have a zero or very low-interest charge and repayments are stretched over 25 to 40 years, including a 5 to 10 year grace period. IDA also provides grants to countries at risk of debt distress.
- In addition to concessional loans and grants, IDA provides significant levels of debt relief to the Heavily Indebted Poor Countries (HIPC), through the Multilateral Debt Relief Initiative (MDRI).

International Finance Corporation (IFC)

- It is the largest global development institution focused exclusively on the private sector in developing countries established in 1956.
- *Various objectives of the IFC are as follows :*
  - To achieve more economic development by encouraging the growth of private enterprise in member countries.
  - To invest in private enterprise in member countries in association with private investors and without a Government guarantee, in cases where sufficient private capital is not available on reasonable terms.
  - To seek for bringing together investment opportunities, private capital of both foreign and domestic origin and experienced management.
  - To stimulate conditions conducive to the flow of private capital (domestic and foreign) into productive investments in member countries.
- IFC investment normally does not exceed 40% of the total investment of the enterprise.
- In case of its investment by equity participation, it does not exceed 25% of the share capital.

Multilateral Investment Guarantee Agency (MIGA)

- It is an international financial institution which offers political risk, insurance and credit enhancement guarantees. Such guarantees help investors protect foreign direct investments against political and non-commercial risks in developing countries.
- MIGA is a member of the World Bank Group and it's headquartered in Washington DC, United States. It was established in 1988 as an investment insurance facility to encourage confident investment in developing countries.
- MIGA's stated mission is "to promote foreign direct investment into developing countries to support economic growth, reduce poverty and improve people's lives". It targets projects that endeavour to create new jobs, develop infrastructure, generate new tax revenues and take advantage of natural resources through sustainable policies and programmes.

International Centre for the Settlement of Investment Disputes (ICSID)

- It is an multilateral, autonomous and international arbitation institution established in 1966 for resolving legal disputes between international investors and nations. It's headquatered in Washington DC.
- It encourages the flow of foreign investment to develop countries through arbitration and conciliation facilities.
- India is not a member of ICSID.
- It was formally organised on 14th October, 1966. When 29 countries signed its Article of Agreement.

International Monetary Fund (IMF)

- It was conceived at a United Nation Conference in Bretton Woods, New Hampshire, United States, in July, 1944.
- The IMF works to foster global monetary cooperation, secure financial stability, facilitate international trade, promote high employment and sustainable economic growth.
- In November 1947, it became special agency of United Nations.
- It's headquartered at Washington DC and its regional offices are at Paris and Geneva.
- It is an organisation of 190 member countries, each of which has representation on the IMF's executive board in proportion to its financial importance. Due to this reason, the most powerful countries in the global economy have the most voting power.
- Various objectives of IMF are as follows :
  - To foster global monetary cooperation.
  - To secure financial stability.

- To facilitate international trade.
- To promote high employment and sustainable economic growth.
- To reduce poverty around the world.

India and the IMF

- India is one of the 44 nations who participated in Bretton Woods Conference, that's why it is member of IMF.
- Finance Minister of India is the ex-officio Governor on the Board of Governors of the IMF. RBI Governor is the Alternate Governor at the IMF.
- India is represented at the IMF by an Executive Director, who also represents three other countries as well, *viz*. Bangladesh, Sri Lanka and Bhutan.

World Trade Organisation (WTO)

- The WTO is the successor to the General Agreement on Tariffs and Trade (GATT), which was created in 1947.
- The Uruguay Round (1986-94) of the GATT led to the creation of WTO. India is a founder member of the GATT and its successor, the WTO. WTO began operations on 1st January, 1995. It's headquarters is in Geneva, Switzerland.
- The Agreement establishing the WTO, commonly known as the "Marrakesh Agreement", was signed in Marrakesh, Morocco in 1994.
- WTO is an international organisation dealing with the rules of trade between nations.
- The main difference between GATT and WTO was that GATT mostly dealt with trade in goods, the WTO and its agreements could not only cover goods but also trade in services and other intellectual properties like trade creations, designs and inventions.
- The WTO has 164 members (including the European Union) and 25 observer governments (like Iran, Iraq, Bhutan, Libya, etc).
- Liberia was the 163rd member on 14th July, 2016 and Afghanistan was the 164th member on 29th July, 2016.

United Nations Conference on Trade and Development (UNCTAD)

- The United Nations Conference on Trade and Development (UNCTAD) was established in 1964.
- It is an intergovernmental body of the United Nations General Assembly for promoting the development-friendly integration of developing countries into the world economy.
- UNCTAD grew from the view that existing institutions like GATT (now WTO), the International Monetary Fund (IMF) and World Bank were not properly organised to handle the particular problems of developing countries.
- UNCTAD's objective is to maximise the trade, investment and development opportunities of developing countries and assist them in their efforts to integrate into the world economy on an equitable basis.
- Various functions of UNCTAD are as follows :
  - It functions as a forum for intergovernmental deliberations, supported by discussions with experts and exchanges of experience, aimed at consensus building.
  - It undertakes research, policy analysis and data collection for the debates of government representatives and experts.
  - It provides technical assistance tailored to the specific requirements of developing countries, with special attention to the needs of the least developed countries and of economies in transition.

World Economic Forum (WEF)

- It is a Swiss non-profit foundation established in 1971, based in Geneva, Switzerland. It is recognised by the Swiss authorities as the international institution for public-private cooperation.
- Its mission is committed to improve the state of the world by engaging business, political, academic and other leaders of society to shape global, regional and industry agendas.

G-7

- G-7 is organisation of 7 non-socialist countries, which were highly industrialised in the world.
- G-7 includes USA, Canada, Germany, Britain, France, Italy and Japan. After adopting free market policies in economy, Russia was also made member of the organisation in June, 1997. However, in 2014 after Russian invasion of Ukraine, it was expelled from G-7.

G-20

- The G-20 is an informal group of 19 countries and the European Union, with representatives of the International Monetary Fund and the World Bank.
- The G-20 membership comprises a mix of the world's largest advanced and emerging economies, representing about two-thirds of the world's population, 85% of global Gross Domestic Product, 80% of global investment and over 75% of global trade.
- Its origin can be traced back to the 1997-1999 Asian Financial Crisis.

- This was a ministerial-level forum which emerged after G-7 invited both developed and developing economies.
- The Finance Ministers and Central Bank Governors began meeting in 1999.
- The members of the G-20 are Argentina, Australia, Brazil, Canada, China, France, Germany, India, Indonesia, Italy, Japan, Republic of Korea, Mexico, Russia, Saudi Arabia, South Africa, Turkey, the United Kingdom, the United States, and the European Union.
- Spain as a permanent, non-member invitee, also attends leader summits.

International Labour Organisation (ILO)

- It was established in 1919 by the Treaty of Versailles as an affiliated agency of the League of Nations.
- It became the first affiliated specialised agency of the United Nations in 1946. Its headquarter is in Geneva, Switzerland.
- It promotes internationally recognised human and labour rights.
- Its founding mission is 'Social justice is essential to universal and lasting peace.'
- The eight-core conventions of the ILO are :
  - Forced Labour Convention (No. 29)
  - Abolition of Forced Labour Convention (No.105)
  - Equal Remuneration Convention (No.100)
  - Discrimination (Employment Occupation) Convention (No.111)
  - Minimum Age Convention (No.138)
  - Worst forms of Child Labour Convention (No.182)
  - Freedom of Association and Protection of Right to Organised Convention (No.87)
  - Right to Organise and Collective Bargaining Convention (No.98)

Asia-Pacific Economic Cooperation (APEC)

- It is a regional economic forum to promote sustainable growth and better economic relations among the member countries or economies. It was established in 1989.
- India is not a member of APEC. Its members are Australia, Brunei, Canada, Chile, China, Hong Kong, Indonesia, Japan, South Korea, Malaysia, Mexico, New Zealand, Papua New Guinea, Peru, Philippines, Russia, Singapore, Chinese Taipei, Thailand, Vietnam and the United States.

India-Brazil-South Africa (IBSA)

- It is a international group promoting international cooperation between India, Brazil and South Africa.
- It was created to promote South cooperation and build consensus on the issue of international importance.
- It represents an important pole for galvanising cooperation among developing countries.

Brazil-Russia-India-China-South Africa (BRICS)

- BRICS is the acronym for an association of 5 major emerging national economies i.e., Brazil, Russia, India, China and South Africa. The BRICS First Summit was held in Yekaterinburg, Russia on 16th June, 2009 and the term was coined by economist Jim O'Neill.
- The 15th Summit of BRICS was held in Johannesburg, South Africa from 22nd-24th August, 2023.

South Asian Association for Regional Cooperation (SAARC)

- It was founded in 1985 and dedicated to economic, technological, social and cultural development emphasising collective self-reliance.
- Its member countries are Afghanistan, Bangladesh, Bhutan, India, Maldives, Nepal, Pakistan and Sri Lanka.
- It promotes the welfare of the people of South Asia and to improve their quality of life.
- It strengthen cooperation among themselves in international forums on matters of common interest.
- It was established to contribute to mutual trust, understanding and appreciation of one another's problems.

Association of South-East Asian Nations (ASEAN)

- It was established in 1967 in Bangkok, (Thailand) by Indonesia, Malaysia, Philippines, Singapore and Thailand. As of 2024, it has 10 member (Apart from founding members Brunei, Vietnam, Lao PDR, Myanmar and Cambodia). It was established to promote active collaboration and mutual assistance on matters of common interest in the economic, social, technical, scientific and administrative field.
- To promote South-East Asian studies.
- To promote regional peace and stability through abiding respect for justice and the rule of law in the relationship among countries of the region and adherence to the principles of the UN Charter.

International Financial Institutions

Some important international financial institutions are as follows :

Bank for International Settlements (BIS)

- It is an inter-governmental organisation of Central Banks which "fosters international monetary and financial cooperation and serves as a bank for Central Banks."
- It is not accountable to any National Government, headquartered at Basel, Switzerland.
- The mission of the Bank for International Settlements (BIS) is to serve Central Banks in their pursuit of monetary and financial stability, to foster international cooperation in those areas and to act as a bank for Central Banks.
- The Basel Committee for Banking Supervision (BCBS), while technically separate from the BIS, is a closely associated international forum for financial regulation.
- The BCBS is responsible for the Basel Accords, which recommend capital requirements and other banking regulations that are widely implemented by National Governments. The BIS also conducts research on economic issues and publishes reports.

European Central Bank (ECB)

- It is the Central Bank responsible for monetary policy of those European Union (EU) member countries which have adopted the euro currency. This region is known as the Eurozone and currently comprises 19 members.
- The principal goal of the ECB is to maintain price stability in the Euro area, thus helping preserve the purchasing power of the Euro. It is the Central Bank of the combined Eurozone.
- ECB was founded on 1st June, 1998.
- It's headquartered in Frankfurt, Germany. It has been responsible for monetary policy in the Euro area since, 1st January, 1999.
- The ECB coordinates EU monetary policy, including setting the region's target interest rates and controlling the supply of the Euro common currency.
- The ECB's primary mandate is to achieve price stability through low inflation.

Asian Infrastructure Investment Bank (AIIB)

- It is a multilateral development bank with a mission to improve social and economic outcomes in Asia.
- It is headquartered in Beijing and began its operations in January, 2016.
- It is established by the AIIB Articles of Agreement (entered into force on 25th December, 2015) which is a multilateral treaty. The Parties (57 founding members) to agreement comprise the Membership of the Bank.
- The members of the bank have now grown to 97 approved members worldwide. There are 27 prospective members including Armenia, Lebanon, Brazil, South Africa, Greece, etc.
- Fourteen of the G-20 nations are AIIB members including France, Germany, India, Italy and the United Kingdom.

Asian Development Bank (ADB)

- It is a regional development bank established on 19th December, 1966.
- ADB now has 68 members, 49 from within Asia. ADB is headquartered in Manila, Philippines.
- It aims to promote social and economic development in Asia.
- ADB is committed to achieving a prosperous, inclusive, resilient and sustainable Asia and the Pacific, while sustaining its efforts to eradicate extreme poverty.

India and the ADB

- India's act of coordination with this bank is done by Finance Ministry.
- As of 31st December, 2020, ADB's five largest shareholders are Japan and the United States (each with 15.6% of total shares), the People's Republic of China (6.4%), India (6.3%), and Australia (5.8%).

New Development Bank (NDB)

- It is a multilateral development bank jointly founded by the BRICS countries at the 6th BRICS Summit in Fortaleza, Brazil in 2014.
- It was formed to support infrastructure and sustainable development efforts in BRICS and other undeserved, emerging economies for faster development through innovation and cutting-edge technology.
- Its headquarters is at Shanghai, China and it is also known as the BRICS bank.
- In 2018, the NDB received observer status in the United Nations General Assembly (UNGA), establishing a firm basis for active and fruitful cooperation with the UN.

Extra Facts From Tamil Nadu Board and NIOS

Facilities offered by International Monetary Fund (IMF)

1. **Basic Credit Facility** The IMF provides financial assistance to its member nations to overcome their temporary difficulties relating to balance of payments. A member nation can purchase from the Fund other currencies or SDRs, in exchange for its own currency, to finance payment deficits.
2. **Reserve Tranche** A member can unconditionally borrow from the Fund in a year equal to 25% of its quota. This unconditional borrowing right is called the reserve tranche.
3. **Extended Fund Facility** Under this arrangement, the IMF provides additional borrowing facility up to 140% of the member's quota, over and above the basic credit facility.
4. **Compensatory Financing Facility** Under this arrangement, the IMF provides additional financial assistance to the member countries, particularly primary-producing countries facing a shortfall in export earnings and fluctuations in the cost of cereal inputs.
5. **Buffer Stock Facility** To help the primary goods-producing countries to finance contributions to buffer stock arrangements for the stabilisation of primary product prices.
6. **Supplementary Financing Facility** Under the supplementary financing facility, the IMF makes temporary arrangements to provide supplementary financial assistance to member countries facing payment problems relating to their present quota sizes.
7. **Structural Adjustment Facility** To provide an additional Balance of Payments (BoP) assistance on concessional terms to the poorer member countries.

- **Special Drawing Rights (SDR)** It is a form of international reserves created by the IMF in 1969 to solve the problem of international liquidity. They are allocated to the IMF members in proportion to their Fund quotas. SDRs are used as a means of payment by Fund members to meet the balance of payments deficits and their total reserve position with the Fund. It acts both as an international unit of account and a means of payment.

World Trade Organisation (WTO)

- The Dunkel Draft, formulated by Arthur Dunkel, its Secretary General became the base for WTO.

Major WTO Agreements

1. **Agreement on Trade-Related Intellectual Property Rights (TRIPs)** It provides for granting product patents instead of process patents. The period of protection will be 20 years for patents, 50 years for copy rights, 7 years for trade marks and 10 years for layout designs.
2. **Agreement on Trade-Related Investment Measures (TRIMs)** It calls for introducing equal treatment for foreign companies on par with national companies in the context of investment.
3. **General Agreement on Trade in Services (GATS)** : It is the first multilateral set of rules covering trade in services like banking, insurance, transportation, communication, etc. Under this all member countries are supposed to extend MFN (Most Favoured Nation) status to all other countries without any discrimination.
4. **Phasing out of the Multi Fibre Agreement (MFA)** It imposed quotas on the export of textiles by developing nations to developed countries.
5. **Agreement on Agriculture** It calls for tariff cuts and subsidy reduction in the field of agricultural trade.

Appendix

Committees/Commissions Related to Indian Economy

Committees/Commissions	Years	Related Subjects
Kothari Commission	1964	Reforms in education systems
Basel Committee	1974	Reforms in banking sector
Tandon Committee	1974	System of working capital financing by banks
SP Talwar	1975	Restructuring of weak public sector bank
Dantwala Committee	1977	Unemployment estimation in the country
Shivraman Committee	1979	Establishment of NABARD
Marathe Committee	1982	Recommendation for urban cooperative banks
Sukhamoy Chakravarty Committee	1982	To assess the functioning of the Indian monetary system
Hanumant Rao Committee	1983	Fertilisers
Vaghul Committee	1987	Money market in India
Khusro Committee	1989	Agricultural credit system
Goiporia Committee	1990	Improvement in the customer service at primary (urban) cooperative banks
Raja Chelliah Committee	1991	Tax reforms
Narasimham Committee	1991	Banking sector reforms
Rekhi Committee	1992	Indirect taxes
Jankiramanan Committee	1992	Securities transaction
GV Ramakrishna Committee	1993	On disinvestment
Malhotra Committee	1993	Broad framework of insurance sector
NN Vohra Committee	1993	Relation (nexus) of politicians with criminals
Goswami Committee	1993	Industrial sickness in India
RV Gupta Committee	1995	Small savings and agricultural credit
Ajit Kumar Committee	1997	Army Pay Scales

Committees/Commissions	Years	Related Subjects
Abid Hussain Committee	1997	On Small Scale Industries
Chandratre Committee	1997	Security analysis and investment
Mahajan Committee	1997	Sugar industry
Meera Seth Committee	1997	Development of handlooms
Tarapore Committee	1997	Report on capital account convertibility
UK Sharma Committee	1998	NABARD's role in RRB
Vasudev Committee	1998	NBFC sector reforms
JS Verma Committee	1999	Current account carry forward practice
Kumarmanglam Birla Report	1999	Corporate governance
SN Verma Committee	1999	Restructuring the Commercial Banks
Dave Committee	2000	Pension scheme for unorganised sector
YB Reddy Committee	2001	Review of Income Tax Rebates
Abhijit Sen Committee	2002	Long Term Food Policy
Sapta Rishi Committee	2002	Development of domestic tea
Mashelkar Committee	2003	Auto Fuel Policy
Udesh Kohli Committee	2003	Analyse fund requirement in power sector
JJ Irani Committee	2004	Company Law Reforms
Swaminathan Committee	2004	To find the problems faced by the farmers
Rakesh Mohan Committee	2004	Improvement the financial sector
Suresh Tendulkar Committee	2005	Redefining poverty line and its calculation formula
Shuglu Committee	2006	Sardar Sarovar Rehabilitation

Committees/Commissions	Years	Related Subjects
Percy Mistry Committee	2007	Making Mumbai an international financial capital
BK Chaturvedi Committee	2008	Financial condition of oil companies
Bhurela Committee	2010	Increase in motor vehicle tax
KC Chakrabarty Committee	2011	To analyse the financial condition of the Regional Rural Banks in India
C Babu Rajiv Committee	2012	Reforms in Ship Act, 1908 and Ship Trust Act, 1963
Kelkar Committee	2012	Tax structure reforms
C Rangarajan Committee	2012	To review the methodology for measurement of poverty
Deepak Parekh Committee	2012	To financing infrastructure through PPP model
Raghuram Rajan Committee	2012	Central assistance to the state
Urjit Patel Committee	2013	Monetary policy
Som Committee	2013	New income tax structure
Dhanuka Committee	2013	Current capital market regulations
Chandra Shekhar Committee	2013	Venture capital
Nachiket Mor Committee	2013	Committee on comprehensive financial services for small businesses and low income households
MB Shah Committee	2014	Enquiry on illegal iron and manganese ore mining
PJ Nayak Committee	2014	To evaluate governance of board of banks and examine criteria to select directors, as well as their term
Ak Mathur Commission	2014	Seventh Pay Commission
K Kasturirangan Committee	2017	To head Drafting Committee of National Education Policy
Bimal Jalan Committee	2018	To decide the appropriate level of reserves that the RBI should hold
Malegam Committee	2018	Rising incidents of fraud and classification of bad loans
Prasad Panel	2018	International trade and services
Kirit Parikh Committee	2022	Review the gas pricing formula

Report/Index and Issuing Body

Report/Index	Issuing body
World Development Report	World Bank
Global Economic Outlook Report	World Bank
Ease of Living Index	World Bank
Global Finance Stability Report	International Monetary Fund
World Economic Outlook Report	International Monetary Fund
Global Competitiveness Report	World Economic Forum
Environment Protection Index	World Economic Forum
Human Capital Index	World Bank
Global Gender Gap Index	World Economic Forum
Global Education Monitoring Report	UNESCO
Gender Inequality Index	UNDP
Global Hunger Index	Concern Worldwide and Welthungerhilfe
Children Climate Risk Index	UNICEF
Hunger Hotspot Report	World Food Programme, Food and Agriculture organsation (FAO)
Global Cyber Security Index	International Telecommunication Union
Global Liveability Index	Economist Intelligence Unit
Report on Gobal Remittance	World Bank
World Press Freedom Index	Reporters Without Borders
World Happiness' Report	UN Sustainable Development Solutions Network
Trade and Development Report	UNCTAD
Corruption Perception Index	Transparency International
World Investment Report	UNCTAD
Technology and Innovation Report	UNCTAD
Human Development Index	UNDP
Climate Change Performance Index	New Climate Institute/ Climate Action Network
Global Innovation Index	(WIPO) World Intellectual Property Organisation
Digital Quality of Life Index	Surfshark
SDG India Index	NITI Aayog
India Innovation Index	NITI Aayog
Poverty and Shared Prosperity Report	World Bank

Certification Mark's in India

- **ISI Mark:** It is a standards-compliance mark for industrial products in India since 1955. The mark certifies that a product conforms to an Indian Standard (IS) developed by the **Bureau of Indian Standards** (BIS), the National Standards body of India. The ISI mark is mandatory for certain products to be sold in India, such as many of the electrical appliances and other household products.
- **FPO Mark** It is a certification mark mandatory on all processed fruit products sold in India such as packaged fruit beverages, fruit-jams, squashes, pickles, dehydrated fruit products and fruit extracts. The mark got a mandatory status after the Food Safety and Standards Act of 2006.
- **AGMark** It is a certification mark employed on agricultural products in India, assuring that they conform to a set of standards approved by the Directorate of Marketing and Inspection under Ministry of Agricultural and Farmers Welfare. The AGMark Head Office is at Faridabad (Haryana). It is legally enforced in India by the Agricultural Produce (Grading and Marking) Act of 1937 (amended in 1986). The present AGMark standards cover quality guidelines for 224 different commodities.
- **BS Mark** It is certification for regulating the output of air pollutants from internal combustion engine and spark-ignition engine equipment, including motor vehicles. Vehicle emission norms were introduced in India in 1991 for petrol and in 1992 for diesel vehicles. Since 2000, Euro norms are followed in India under the name Bharat Stage Emission Standards for four wheeled vehicles. Bharat Stage III norms have been enforced across India since October 2010.
- **BIS Hallmark** It is a hallmarking system for gold as well as silver jewellery sold in India certifying the purity of the metal. The BIS system of hallmarking of gold jewellery began in April 2000. BIS introduced hallmarking for silver jewellery in December 2005 under BIS 2112, the standard specification for hallmarking of silver.
- **India Organic Mark** It is a certification mark for organically farmed food products manufactured in India. The certification mark certifies that an organic food product conforms to the National Standards for Organic Products established in 2000. The certification is issued by testing centres accredited by the Agricultural and Processed Food Products Export Development Authority (APEDA) under the National Programme for Organic Production of the Government of India. Even though the standards are in effect since 2000, the certification scheme and hence, the certification mark came into existence in 2002.
- **Eco Mark** It is a certification mark issued by the Bureau of Indian Standards (the National Standards Organisation of India) to products conforming to a set of standards aimed at the least impact on the ecosystem. The marking scheme was started in 1991. Under this Scheme, the Government of India has notified the final criteria for the 17 product categories.
- **Silk Mark** It is a certification mark in India for silk textiles. The certification is managed by the 'Silk Mark Organisation of India', a society set up by the state-controlled Central Silk Board of India. The certification scheme was founded by the Central Silk Board in 2004.
- **Vegetarian Mark** The symbol is in effect following the Food Safety and Standards (Packaging and Labeling) Act of 2006, received a mandatory status after the framing of the respective regulations (Food Safety and Standards (Packaging and Labeling) Regulation in 2011. According to the law, vegetarian food should be identified by a green symbol and non-vegetarian food with a brown symbol.
- **FSSAI Mark** The Food Safety and Standards Authority of India (FSSAI) has been established under Food Safety and Standards, 2006 which consolidates various acts and orders that handle food related issues in various ministries and departments. FSSAI has been created for laying down science based standards for articles of food and to regulate their manufacture, storage, distribution, sale and import to ensure availability of safe and wholesome food for human consumption.

Glossary

- **Invisibles** An invisible trade is an international transaction that does not include an exchange of tangible goods. Customer service outsourcing, overseas banking transactions, the medical tourism industry, etc are the examples of invisible trade. Any transaction that is associated with a value but not with physical goods could be called an invisible trade.
- **De-reservation** It implies opening up of those industries for the private sector that were exclusively reserved for the government sector. It is one of the important policies that was followed under the policy of privatisation as a part of the New Economic Reforms.
- **Devaluation** It is an official lowering of the value of a country's currency within a fixed exchange-rate system, in which a monetary authority formally sets a lower exchange rate of the national currency in relation to a foreign reference currency or currency basket. The opposite of devaluation, a change in the exchange rate making the domestic currency more expensive, is called a revaluation.
- **Opportunity Cost** It represents the potential benefits lacked by an individual, investor or business while choosing one alternative over another. Understanding the potential missed opportunities when a business or individual chooses one investment over another allows for better decision-making.
- **Import Substitution** It is a strategy under trade policy that abolishes the import of foreign products and encourages production in the domestic market. The purpose of this policy is to change the economic structure of the country by replacing foreign goods with domestic goods.
- **Tariff** A tariff, is a tax levied on an imported good. These are of two types. A 'unit' or specific tariff is a tax levied as a fixed charge for each unit of a good that is imported. e.g., $300 per tonne of imported steel. An 'ad valorem' tariff is levied as a proportion of the value of imported goods.
- **Consumption Basket** A basket of goods is a constant set of general goods produced in an economy whose prices are tracked over time. The basket is used to measure inflation over time, such as with the Consumer Price Index (CPI).
- **Bureau of Energy Efficiency** The Government of India set up Bureau of Energy Efficiency (BEE) on 1st March, 2002 under the provisions of the Energy Conservation Act, 2001. Its aim is to assist in developing policies and strategies with a thrust on self-regulation and market principles, within the overall framework of the Energy Conservation Act, 2001.
- **Cascading Effect** This effect is when there is a tax on tax levied on a product at every step of the sale. The tax is levied on a value that includes tax paid by the previous buyer, thus, making the end consumer pay 'tax on already paid tax'.
- **Commercialisation of Agriculture** Commercialisation of agriculture is a phenomenon where agriculture is governed by commercial consideration i.e. certain specialised crops began to be grown not for consumption in village but for sale in national and even in international market. Commercialisation of agriculture in India began during the British rule.
- **Demographic Transition** It is a phenomenon and theory which refers to the historical shift from high birth rates and high death rates in societies with minimal technology, education (especially of women) and economic development, to low birth rates and low death rates in societies with advanced technology, education and economic development, as well as the stages between these two scenarios.
- **Quantitative Restrictions** Quantitative restrictions are the limits imposed on the quantity of goods which are exported and imported in the global market. These restrictions discourage the imports of goods and protect the domestically produced goods from competition. But these restrictions were abolished by World Trade Organisation (WTO) to facilitate world trade.
- **Balance of Payment** (BOP) It is also known as the Balance of International Payments. It is a statement of all transactions made between entities in one country and the rest of the world over a defined period, such as a quarter or a year. It summarises all transactions that a country's individuals, companies and government bodies complete with individuals, companies and government bodies outside the country.
- **Disinvestment** It is when governments or organisations sell or liquidate assets or subsidiaries. Disinvestments can take the form of divestment or a reduction of Capital Expenditures (CapEx). Disinvestment is carried out for a variety of reasons, such as strategic, political or environmental. After 1991, disinvestment began in India.
- **Foreign Institutional Investors** (FIIs) These are an institutional, individual or group entity seeking to invest in the economy of a country other than where the entity is headquartered. FIIs are important to emerging economies because they bring funds and capital to businesses in developing countries.